TABLE OF CONTENTS

INTRODUCTION

Background

The Department of Homeland Security has the vital mission of protecting the homeland, its citizens, and our nation's way of life from a wide range of threats that shape our strategic environment.[1] The threats from terrorism, cyber-attacks, pandemics and catastrophic natural disasters are real and "pose the greatest risk to the security of the Nation."[2] The potential impact of these threats are so complicated that no single organization, department, or agency has the capabilities, resources, authority, or expertise needed to prevent, protect against, mitigate, respond to, and recover from an event.[3] Many of the capabilities needed to protect our citizens reside within a variety of organizations across Federal, State, local, tribal governments and the private and non-governmental sectors.[4] Success requires a unified effort that integrates and synchronizes all of our national capabilities to maximize efficiencies and effectiveness when crafting the homeland security strategy for an uncertain future.

> Homeland security describes the intersection of evolving threats and hazards with traditional governmental and civic responsibilities for civil defense, emergency response, law enforcement, customs, border control, and immigration. In combining these responsibilities, homeland security breaks down longstanding stovepipes of activity that could be exploited by those seeking to harm America. Homeland security also creates a greater emphasis on the need for joint actions and efforts across previously discrete elements of government and society.[5]

---

[1] U.S. President (Obama), *National Security Strategy* (Washington DC: Government Printing Office, May 2010), 1-3.

[2] U.S. Department of Homeland Security, *National Preparedness Goal*, First Edition, Government Printing Office (Washington D.C., 2011), A-2.

[3] Professor L. Erik Kjonnerod, "Organizing the Stovepipes: Interagency thru WOG-WON to Whole of Planet" (presentation at the Center of Applied Strategic Learning, Fort McNair, Washington D.C., July 2011).

[4] *National Preparedness Goal*, A-2.

[5] U.S. Department of Homeland Security, *Quadrennial Homeland Security Review Report*, Government Printing Office (Washington, D.C., 2010), viii.

The Homeland Security Act of 2002 established the Department of Homeland Security as an executive department within the Federal government following the terrorist attacks of September 11, 2001.[6] Prior to this legislation, homeland security activities were dispersed among dozens of Federal agencies and thousands of first responders at the State and local levels across the Nation. The Department of Homeland Security's original mission[7] was to:

(a) Prevent terrorist attacks within the United States;
(b) Reduce the vulnerability of the United States to terrorism;
(c) Minimize the damage, and assist in the recovery, from terrorist attacks that occur within the United States;
(d) Carry out all functions of entities transferred to the Department, including by acting as a focal point regarding natural and manmade crises and emergency planning;
(e) Ensure that the functions of the agencies and sub-division within the Department that are not related directly to securing the homeland are not diminished or neglected except by a specific Act of Congress;
(f) Ensure that the overall economic security of the United States is not diminished by efforts, activities, and programs aimed at securing the homeland; and
(g) Monitor connections between illegal drug trafficking and terrorism, coordinate efforts to sever such connections, and otherwise contribute to efforts to interdict illegal drug trafficking.[8]

From these general roles and missions, the Department's leadership had to link strategy to performance and resource planning to effectively communicate their strategic direction and purpose to the organization.

The Issue

In March 2003, the Department of Homeland Security was transferred 22 separate federal departments and agencies to accomplish its mission. Of its 22 components, only the U.S. Coast Guard (USCG), the U.S. Secret Service (USSS) and the Federal

---

[6] U.S. Department of Homeland Security, *Homeland Security Act of 2002*, P.L. 107-296, 116 Stat. 2135, Government Printing Office (Washington, D.C., 2002), 8.
[7] The 2010 Quandrennial Homeland Security Review Report and 2012 Department of Homeland Security Strategic Plan has modified the Department's mission and will be discussed in Chapter 2.
[8] Homeland Security Act of 2002, 8.

Emergency Management Agency (FEMA) were transferred as whole organizations. This merger represents one of the largest reorganizations of the National Security infrastructure since the National Security Act of 1947 that lead to the creation of the Department of Defense and the Joint Staff. Nearly a decade later, the Department of Homeland Security still has many challenges that affect its ability to accomplish its homeland security mission. Among these challenges is the Department's inability to craft a strategy for how its internal management practices will be conducted among its 22 disparate components based upon their diverse missions, different resource requirements and distinct organizational cultures. Developing an integrated management system is a way to build a more cohesive, efficient and effective Department.[9] According to a recent U.S. Government Accountability Office report, the Department of Homeland Security has made progress in maturing the organization; however, its evolution remains at "high risk" due to its program weaknesses and management issues that hinder the implementation of efforts such as leading and coordinating the homeland security enterprise; implementing and integrating management functions for results; and strategically managing risk and assessing homeland security efforts.[10]

Another challenge is the variety of organizations, capabilities, and authorities the Department of Homeland Security must integrate into the national planning effort to build national security capacity to address the future threats and hazards that confront the

---

[9] U.S. Department of Homeland Security, "Written testimony of DHS Management Under Secretary for a House Homeland Security Subcommittee on Oversight, Investigations, and Management hearing on management integration," Department of Homeland Security, http://www.dhs.gov/news/2012/02/29/written-testimony-dhs-management-under-secretary-house-homeland-security (accessed September 7, 2012).

[10] United States, Department of Homeland Security Progress Made and Work Remaining in Implementing Homeland Security Missions 10 Years After 9/11: Report to Congressional Requesters, U.S. Government Accountability Office (GAO-11-881), Government Printing Office (Washington, D.C., 2011), 1.

Nation. These capabilities and authorities include the integration of law enforcement, information sharing, emergency response, civil defense and cyber security assets across the Nation. By far the largest organization with the most capabilities resides within the Department of Defense; while most of the authorities needed for joint action overlap numerous Federal departments, State and local agencies, and private sector stakeholders. In order to maximize the Department of Homeland Security's ability to share the security burden, President George W. Bush signed Homeland Security Presidential Directive-5 (HSPD-5) and Homeland Security Presidential Directive-8 (HSPD-8), while President Barack Obama signed Presidential Policy Directive-8 (PPD-8). In February 2003, President Bush signed HSPD-5, *Management of Domestic Incidents* which directed cooperative action between the Department of Defense and Department of Homeland Security to enhance the ability of the military to provide defense support to civil authorities for domestic incidents by "establishing a single, comprehensive national incident management system."[11] In relation to HSPD-5, President Bush signed HSPD-8, *National Preparedness* which established the Secretary of the Department of Homeland Security as the "principal Federal official for coordinating the implementation of all-hazards preparedness in the United States."[12] In March 2011, President Obama signed PPD-8, *National Preparedness* which built upon the requirements outlined in HSPD-8 and directed the Department of Homeland Security to lead all coordination and collaboration efforts among Federal, State, local, tribal governments and the private and

---

[11] George W. Bush, "Homeland Security Presidential Directive/HSPD-5 Management of Domestic Incidents," Administration of George W. Bush, 2003, http://www.gpo.gov/fdsys/pkg/PPP-2003-book1/pdf/PPP-2003-book1-doc-pg229.pdf (accessed July 30, 2012).
[12] George W. Bush, "Homeland Security Presidential Directive/HSPD-8 National Preparedness," Administration of George W. Bush, 2003. http://www.gpo.gov/fdsys/pkg/PPP-2003-book2/pdf/PPP-2003-book2-doc-pg1745.pdf (accessed August 17, 2012).

non-governmental organizations "aimed at facilitating an integrated, all-of-Nation, capabilities-based approach to preparedness."[13] This capability-based approach would be accomplished by developing a National Preparedness Goal, National Preparedness System, Frameworks for Protection, Prevention, Mitigation, Response and Recovery, and associated Interagency Operation Plans. The combination of these documents link national capabilities to the homeland security enterprise and provides a means to identify and remedy capability gaps among the stakeholders. According to a recent U.S. Government Accountability Office report, the Department of Homeland Security must "address gaps and weaknesses in its current operational and implementation efforts, and strengthen the efficiency and effectiveness of those efforts to achieve its full potential."[14] Building partnerships among the homeland security enterprise and across its components is a way for the Department of Homeland Security to identify gaps and reduce the complexity of an event.

Thesis Statement

Despite its wide range of duties that span from aviation and border security to emergency response and from cyber security analysis to chemical facility inspection, the Department of Homeland Security is best understood as a mismatched group of agencies with different cultures and functions lumped together by a common mission to secure the nation from both internal and external threats.[15] There are skeptics who believe this mission may be too hard to accomplish given these existing organizational normative

---

[13] U.S. Department of Homeland Security, "Presidential Policy Directive/PPD-8: National Preparedness," Department of Homeland Security, http://www.dhs.gov/xabout/laws/gc_1215444247124.shtm (accessed July 30, 2012).

[14] Department of Homeland Security Progress Made and Work Remaining in Implementing Homeland Security Missions 10 Years After 9/11: Report to Congressional Requesters, Summary.

[15] U.S. Department of Homeland Security, "About DHS," Department of Homeland Security, http://www.dhs.gov/about-dhs (accessed July 30, 2012).

differences, and the future of Department of Homeland Security is one wrought with bureaucracy and continued inefficiencies. After 10 years in existence, it is time for the Department of Homeland Security to look at its historical symptoms that point to a need for organizational change if it is to remain a viable government department into the future. The Department of Homeland Security must remodel its organizational architecture to include the creation of a Homeland Security Integration Element (similar to that of the Department of Defense [The Joint Staff model]) to act as the focal point for integrating internal Department of Homeland Security operations and facilitating interagency coordination and collaboration with the goal of building a unity of effort across the government departments.

Research Methodology

This paper proposes a conceptual framework for the establishment of a Homeland Security Integration Element within the Department of Homeland Security. This research will address three basic issues: What are the basic functions of the proposed organization? How will the proposed organization improve the internal Department of Homeland Security management systems? How might the proposed organization integrate homeland security efforts across the government? The author will apply the Department of Defense hierarchy and the roles and functions of the Joint Staff to outline the basic structure and functions of the proposed Department of Homeland Security model. The primary methodology for this research is a literature review of strategic documents, Congressional testimony, U.S. Government reports, Presidential directives and orders, manuals and doctrine. This paper will not resolve the conflict between Departmental authorities that require legislative action. However, the author will make recommendations for legislative actions that should be taken to provide the Homeland Security Integration Element with the necessary authorities it needs to discharge its functions. This thesis begins by describing Department of Homeland Security's current organizational structure and capabilities, its internal challenges, conflicts between authorities and the record of previous research regarding attempts to build a unity of effort throughout the government departments. It goes on to analyze the Department of Homeland Security management systems to provide an understanding and appreciation of the manpower, planning, training and resourcing requirements needed for integration within the Department. It likewise will analyze homeland security activities to provide an understanding of the need for interagency coordination and collaboration. Then it will describe the role and functions of the Homeland Security Integration Element and its potential effects on the Department of Homeland Security Headquarters and its components. Finally, the research provides recommendations to enable the creation of the Homeland Security Integration Element and help the Department integrate its management system and homeland security activities to build a unity of effort.

CHAPTER 2: REVIEW OF LITERATURE

Overview

A vast array of literature is written on the Department of Homeland Security and the complexity of its mission to orchestrate a unity of effort among all of the stakeholders in the homeland security enterprise. The homeland security enterprise is defined as "the Federal, State, local, tribal, territorial, nongovernmental, and private-sector entities, as well as individuals, families, and communities who share a common national interest in the safety and security of America and the American population."[1] Similarly, a series of U.S. Government Accountability Office reports document the need for the Department of Homeland Security to take action to improve its internal management practices and to enhance interagency coordination, collaboration and synchronization of capabilities identified within the National Planning Frameworks and Interagency Operation Plans. In this chapter the author will review the current literature as it relates to: U.S. Public Expectations; an overview of the Department of Homeland Security and its organizational structure and capabilities; a review the challenges of the current Departmental model in relation to its conflicts between authorities, policies, and procedures with external organizations; and, a review of the Departments internal management challenges.

U. S. Public Expectations

Managing public expectations is a key factor in influencing the outcome of an event in the homeland security enterprise because an individual's most basic motivational need of food, clothing, shelter and water are put at risk in accordance with Psychologist

---

[1] U.S. Department of Homeland Security, *Quadrennial Homeland Security Review Report*, Government Printing Office (Washington, D.C., 2010), iii.

Abraham Maslow's Theory of Motivation/Hierarchy of Needs. Maslow suggests that all people are motivated by needs. Figure 1 provides a visual depiction of Maslow's model of Hierarchy of Needs.

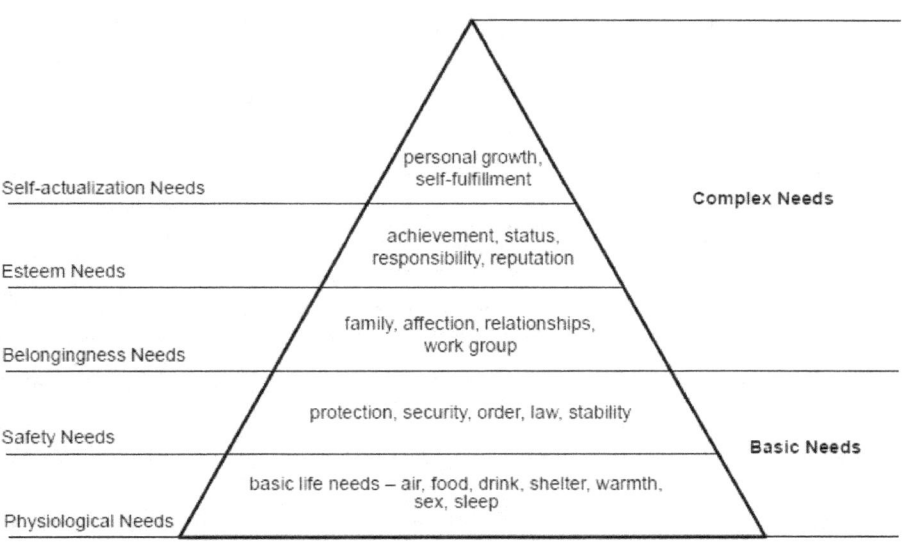

Figure 1. Maslow's Theory of Motivation/Hierarchy of Needs.[2]

Maslow's Hierarchy shows a pyramid divided into five levels with the most basic motivational needs at the bottom and the more complex motivational needs towards the top. Maslow's Theory suggests that only when the lower two levels of the basic motivational needs are satisfied, can an individual move up the pyramid to the next level and return a normal state of being.[3] Meeting an individual's basic motivational needs is where homeland security resides.

Overall, there is little government literature published on managing public expectations in relation to the homeland security enterprise. However, a way to gain insight into public expectations is by examining public opinion polls and news articles taken after major catastrophes such as 9/11, Hurricanes Katrina and Irene, and Super

---

[2] Kendra Cherry, "Psychology: Hierarchy of Needs; The Five Levels of Maslow's Hierarchy of Needs," About.com, http://psychology.about.com/od/theoriesofpersonality/a/hierarchyneeds.htm (accessed December 1, 2012).
[3] Ibid.

Storm Sandy. Major catastrophes can influence U.S. public opinion and trust in government by revealing how well an administration is prepared to prevent, protect, mitigate, respond and recover from an event. In the aftermath of September 11, 2001, Americans placed trust in their Federal government to marshal its resources and respond to the terrorist attacks with military force. Fears of another terrorist attack marked a change in public opinion towards security and led to the creation the Department of Homeland Security and the Patriot Act.[4] The events of 9/11 and the 2001 anthrax attacks[5] lead to billions of tax dollars being devoted to securing the homeland to counter both natural and man-made events. More importantly, the American public and business communities gave up certain civil liberties in exchange for greater security.[6] In August 2005, public opinion of the Federal government would change again in the wake of Hurricane Katrina. The Federal government was criticized for its slow response, poorly integrated capabilities, and "the system, at every level of government, was not well-coordinated, and was overwhelmed in the first few days."[7] The CNN effect further highlighted the ineffectiveness of the government's response by cycling daily video of the aftermath of destruction and human suffering. As a result, the Federal government recognized the importance of managing the dissemination of accurate disaster information about public health, safety, and security through the means of the news media. This unexpected failure also brought into question the government's use of

---

[4] Virgina A. Chanley, "Trust in Government in the Aftermath of 9/11: Determinants and Consequences," *Political Psychology* 23, no. 3 (September 2002): 479.

[5] The Associated Press, "Key events in the anthrax episode," *USATODAY.com*, August 7, 2008, under "Washington News," http://usatoday30.usatoday.com/news/washington/2008-08-06-1546732145_x.htm (accessed February 7, 2013).

[6] Roeliene van Es, "Public Opinions on Security and Civil Liberties in America after the Terrorist Attacks of September 11, 2001," *Social Cosmos* 3, no. 1 (2012), 119.

[7] United States, *The Federal Response to Hurricane Katrina: Lessons Learned*, The White House Office of the Press Secretary, Government Printing Office (Washington D.C., 2006), 19.

billions of dollars to strengthen the emergency preparedness and the public safety response systems. These two major catastrophes helped mold public opinion into a form of "zero tolerance" for government failure. In Congressional testimony, Senator Tom Caper stated, "the Department of Homeland Security, the Department of Defense, and other federal agencies [need] to become better stewards of the taxpayer dollars we entrust them with by improving their financial management practices and systems."[8] Today, the U.S. public expects all levels of government to work together to prevent and protect its citizens from another terrorist attack and be ready to respond, recover and then mitigate the future effects of potential natural and man-made events.

The Department of Homeland Security

The Department of Homeland Security represents the third largest cabinet department in the Federal government behind the Department of Defense and the Department of Veteran Affairs. Secretary Janet Napolitano currently serves as fourth Department head for the Department of Homeland Security. By law, the Secretary is appointed by the President with the consent of the U.S. Senate.[9] The Secretary of Homeland Security also has the responsibility for establishing International Security Cooperation with the countries of Canada and Mexico. The Department's fiscal year 2013 total budget authority is $59.0 billion which is relatively small when compared to the size and mission of the organization.[10] The key elements of the Department of Homeland Security are its structure, business processes, politics, people and culture. The

---

[8] Tom Carper, Senator, U.S. Senate, Senate Homeland Security and Governmental Affairs, Committee, "The Future of Homeland Security," *FDCH Congressional Testimony* (July 12, 2012): Military & Government Collection, EBSCOhost, 2, (accessed July 31, 2012).

[9] U.S. Department of Homeland Security, *Homeland Security Act of 2002*, P.L. 107-296, 116 Stat. 2135, Government Printing Office (Washington, D.C., 2002), 8.

[10] U.S. Department of Homeland Security, *FY 2013 Budget in Brief*, Government Printing Office (Washington, D.C., 2012), 6.

Department of Homeland Security is headquartered at the Navy Annex Complex, Washington D.C., employs approximately 230,000 civil service personnel, contractors and U.S. Coast Guard service members to protect critical domestic lines of communication such as ports, airports, civil populations, economic centers and cyberspace.[11] In addition, the Department of Homeland Security must be ready to respond and recover from natural and manmade events such as hurricanes, earthquakes, tornados and the discharge of a weapon of mass destruction. Most of the Department's components are headquartered at different locations throughout the Nation. The 2010 *Quadrennial Homeland Security Review* and the 2012 *Department of Homeland Security Strategic Plan: FY 2012-2016* refined the Department's mission and activities to: preventing terrorism and enhancing security; securing and managing U.S. borders; enforcing and administering U.S. immigration laws; safeguarding and securing cyberspace; ensuring resilience to disasters; providing essential support to National and economic security; and, mature and strengthen DHS.[12] These refined missions and activities illustrate the evolution the Department is continuing to explore. However, the Department of Homeland Security organizational structure and capabilities did not increase with this change.

Department of Homeland Security Organizational Structure

The Department of Homeland Security was originally organized by directorates which had the responsibility for the integration of the Department's component agencies, such as:

---

[11] Janet Napolitano, Secretary of United States Department of Homeland Security. "DHS Oversight," *FDCH Congressional Testimony* (July 12, 2012): Military & Government Collection, EBSCOhost, 1, (accessed July 31, 2012).

[12] U.S. Department of Homeland Security, *Department of Homeland Security Strategic Plan, Fiscal Years 2012-2016*, Government Printing Office (Washington, D.C., 2012), 2.

[The directorate of] emergency preparedness would oversee domestic disaster response and training. Border security would streamline all port operations. And the S&T directorate would acquire scientific and technological skills, mostly from the private sector. The information analysis directorate was supposed to analyze intelligence from other agencies, including the Central Intelligence Agency (CIA), Federal Bureau of Investigation (FBI), Defense Intelligence Agency (DIA) and National Security Agency (NSA), involving threats to the homeland and vulnerabilities in the nation's infrastructure.[13]

The advantage of the directorate-driven model is it places management emphasis "upon formal procedures and a high degree of structure and control", in a low risk environment.[14] However, the disadvantage of this low-risk style of management is the adverse effects it has on the integration of new ideas, which in turn remain stove piped within an individual directorate.[15] In July 2005, former Secretary of Homeland Security Michael Chertoff initiated a comprehensive review of the Department's structures, policies and operations with the intent of identifying organizational inefficiencies.[16] The findings revealed a need for the Department to improve its internal communication and coordination structure with its components. This led to the creation of an Assistant Secretary for Cyber Security and Telecommunication, an Undersecretary for Policy, a Chief Medical Officer and a U.S. Coast Guard Military Liaison at the Headquarters.[17] Additionally, this review would lead to the Department's change from a directorate driven-model to a component-driven model, establishing the Headquarters element as the central point of focus for integration. The advantage of the component-driven model is it places management emphasis on "a more centralized decision-making structure with

---

[13] Jane Harman, Congresswoman, U.S. House of Representatives, Senate Homeland Security and Governmental Affairs, Committee, "Senator Joseph I. Lieberman holds a hearing on Homeland Security Department's Roles/Missions," *FDCH Political Transcripts (n.d.):* Military & Government Collection, EBSCOhost, 8, (accessed July 31, 2012).

[14] Don Harvey and Donald R. Brown, *An Experiential Approach to Organizational Development: Six Edition* (New Jersey: Prentice Hall, 2001), 35.

[15] Ibid, 36.

[16] U.S. Department of Homeland Security, "Department Six-point Agenda," Department of Homeland Security, http://www.dhs.gov/department-six-point-agenda (accessed October 6, 2012).

[17] Ibid.

problems being referred to the top" and tends to work best in a stable environment.[18] However, the disadvantage of this management model is "planning and decision making are usually concentrated at the top, with coordination done by formal committees" and little input from its subordinate organizations.[19]

In October 2006, President G.W. Bush signed into law the Post-Katrina Emergency Reform Act to correct the organizational failures caused by the Department's slow response to Hurricane Katrina. Under the Post-Katrina Act, the Federal Emergency Management Agency (FEMA) is empowered as the lead agency for all emergency management efforts and the FEMA Administrator is elevated to Deputy Secretary within the Department.[20] What this means is the Federal Emergency Management Agency Administrator has the authority to bypass the Secretary of Homeland Security and has direct access to the President during a national emergency. The 9/11 Commission Act of 2007 introduced another organizational change elevating the Assistant Secretary for Intelligence and Analysis to an Under Secretary level "in order to promote internal information sharing among the intelligence and other personnel of the Department."[21]

In November 2008, the *International Association of Emergency Managers*, a prominent association of emergency managers, made a recommendation to the Obama administration to remove FEMA from the Department of Homeland Security and restore

---

[18] Harvey and Brown, An Experiential Approach, 36.
[19] Ibid.
[20] Congressional Reserch Service, Federal Emergency Management Policy Changes after Hurricane Katrina: A Summary of Statutory Provisions, by the Congressional Research Service, March 2007 (Washington, D.C.: Government Printing Office, 2007), 5.
[21] U.S. Department of Homeland Security, *Implementing Recommendations of the 9/11 Commission Act of 2007*, P.L. 110-53, 121 Stat. 266, Government Printing Office (Washington, D.C., 2007), 8.

the status of the FEMA Administrator to cabinet level position with no success.[22] Figure

2 provides a depiction of the current Department of Homeland Security hierarchy.

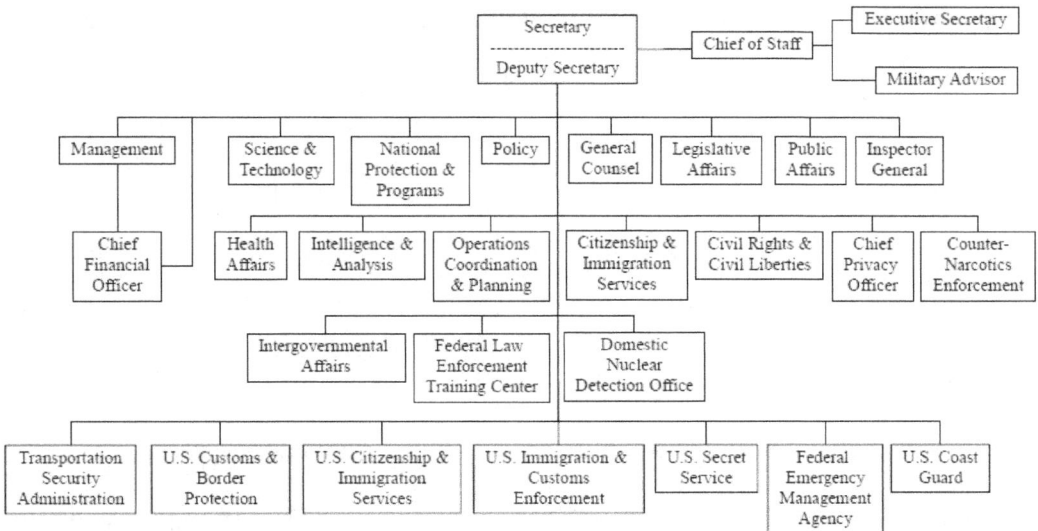

[1] The Consolidated Appropriations Act of 2012 (P.L. 112-74) terminated the Office of Counternarcotic Enforcement and authorized the transfer Of its policy development and coordination responsibilities to the Office of Policy by March 30, 2012.

Figure 2. Department of Homeland Security Organizational Chart.[23]

The Department of Homeland Security coordinates through a structural hierarchy

consisting of political, senior leadership and management at the Headquarters, and

operational personnel within the components. The major component agencies within the

Department of Homeland Security are the Transportation Security Administration, U.S.

Customs & Border Protection, U.S. Citizenship & Immigration Services, U.S.

Immigration & Customs Enforcement, U.S. Secret Service, FEMA and the U.S. Coast

Guard. Of the major component agencies, the Federal Emergency Management Agency

is the only organization with a non-terrorism related mission[24]. The other six major

component agencies primarily focus on law enforcement and counter-terrorism

---

[22] Michael Thomas, "Emergency Managers endorse removing FEMA from DHS," Lighthouse Worldwide Solutions, http://hspolitics.wordpress.com/2008/11/20/emergency-managers-endorse-removing-fema-from-dhs/ (accessed December 7, 2012).
  [23] Department of Homeland Security Strategic Plan, Fiscal Years 2012-2016, 2.
  [24] The Federal Emergency Management Agency's primary purpose to coordinate the federal government's response and recovery from an event.

missions[25] and the remaining 15 smaller agencies[26] report directly to the Department

Headquarters element. Today, Secretary Napolitano's internal priorities continue to

focus on ways "to improve cross-departmental management, strengthen the Department's

workforce and enhance information sharing as goals to mature and strengthen the

Department."[27]

Department of Homeland Security Capabilities

Shortly after the 9/11 terrorist attacks, President G.W. Bush issued Homeland

Security Presidential Directive-5 to link national activities[28] with national capabilities[29] at

all levels of government with the intent to create an integrated approach towards

domestic incident management.[30] This directive requires the Department of Homeland

Security to coordinate with over 100 external agencies that have responsibilities for

national security.[31] According to a Government Accountability Office report there was a

need to improve the "Federal government's capabilities to analyze incident, threat, and

vulnerabilities information obtained from numerous sources and share appropriate,

timely, useful warnings and other information concerning cyber and physical threats to

---

[25] The primary purpose of these organizations is to prevent and protect the nation from threats.

[26] The 15 smaller agencies are Science & Technology, National Protection and Programs, Policy, Legislative Affairs, Public Affairs, Health Affairs, Intelligence and Analysis, Operations Coordination and Planning, Citizenship and Immigration Services, Civil Rights and Civil Liberties, Chief Privacy Officer, Counter Narcotics Enforcement, Intergovernmental Affairs, Federal Law Enforcement Training Center and Domestic Nuclear Detection Office.

[27] Department of Homeland Security Strategic Plan, Fiscal Years 2012-2016, 24.

[28] National activities are those functions needed to maintain protection, security, order , law, and stability.

[29] National capabilities are discussed in Figure 3.

[30] George W. Bush, "Homeland Security Presidential Directive/HSPD-5 Management of Domestic Incidents," White House Office of the Press Secretary, http://www.fas.org/irp/offdocs/nspd/hspd-5.html (accessed July 30, 2012).

[31] William L. Waugh, Jr., "The Future of Homeland Security," (presentation at the FEMA Higher Education Conference, Emmitsburg, MD, June 7-9, 2005).

entities, State and local government, and the private sector."[32] In order to enable the

Department to operate more effectively, the Secretary of Homeland Security tasked the

Office of Operations, Coordination and Planning to establish the National Operations

Center within the Headquarters to manage the flow of information across the homeland

security enterprise. The National Operations Center will be further discussed in

Chapter 4. Sequentially, President Bush issued Homeland Security Presidential

Directive-8, *National Preparedness* which tasked the Department with the development

of a national domestic all-hazards preparedness goal, which would serve as a mechanism

for the "improved delivery of Federal preparedness assistance [capabilities] to State and

local governments."[33] In turn, President Barrack Obama took the next step to the Bush

Administration's HSPD-8 by issuing Presidential Policy Directive-8, *National*

Preparedness which directed the development of a National Preparedness Goal, National

Preparedness System, Frameworks for Protection, Prevention, Mitigation, Response and

Recovery, and associated Interagency Operation Plans. The Homeland Security

Enterprise is currently working to completing the five National Frameworks.

A product of Homeland Security Presidential Directive-8[34] and later Presidential

Policy Directive-8[35] was the development of core capabilities that are deemed critical for

---

[32] United States, *Homeland Security: Information Sharing Responsibilities, Challenges, and Key Management Issues,* U.S. Government Accountability Office (GAO-03-1165T), Government Printing Office (Washington, D.C., 2003), 2.

[33] George W. Bush, "Homeland Security Presidential Directive/HSPD-8 National Preparedness," White House Office of the Press Secretary, http://www.fas.org/irp/offdocs/nspd/hspd-8 html (accessed August 17, 2012).

[34] Initated by the Bush Adminstration.

[35] The Obama Adminstration's next step to the Bush Adminstration's Homeland Security Presidential Directive-8.

the execution of five common mission areas.[36] Figure 3 provides a depiction of the Core

Capabilities by Mission Area.

Prevention	Protection	Mitigation	Response	Recovery
Planning				
Public Information and Warning				
Operational Coordination				
Forensics and Attribution Intelligence and Information Sharing Interdiction and Disruption Screening, Search, and Detection	Access Control and Identity Verification Cybersecurity Intelligence and Information Sharing Interdiction and Disruption Physical Protective Measures Risk Management for Protection Programs and Activities Screening, Search, and Detection Supply Chain Integrity and Security	Community Resilience Long-term Vulnerability Reduction Risk and Disaster Resilience Assessment Threats and Hazard Identification	Critical Transportation Environmental Response/Health and Safety Fatality Management Services Infrastructure Systems Mass Care Services Mass Search and Rescue Operations On-scene Security and Protection Operational Communications Public and Private Services and Resources Public Health and Medical Services Situational Assessment	Economic Recovery Health and Social Services Housing Infrastructure Systems Natural and Cultural Resources

Figure 3. Core Capabilities by Mission Area.[37]

The five common mission areas are defined as prevention, protection, mitigation,

response, and recovery. Within each mission area is a list of 31 core capabilities that

reside within a variety of organizations across Federal, State, local, tribal governments

and the private sector. The three cross-cutting core capabilities that are needed to

integrate the five mission areas are planning, public information and warning, and

operational coordination. Additionally, each core capability is linked to a performance

objective called capability targets.[38] The capability targets guide the "allocation of

---

[36] U.S. Department of Homeland Security, *National Preparedness Goal*, First Edition, Government Printing Office (Washington D.C., 2011), 2.

[37] Ibid.

[38] Capability targets serve as the basis for the development of performance measures to track national progress.

resources in support of our national preparedness".[39] Of the 31 core capabilities, the 2012 Department of Homeland Security *National Preparedness Report* ranks "cyber security" and "recovery focused" capabilities as areas of weakness for meeting the *National Preparedness Goal.*[40] Likewise the same report identifies "planning", one of the three cross-cutting core capabilities, as a national function that can be improved.[41]

The Federal Response to Hurricane Katrina: Lessons Learned report indicated a need to improve the operational management capabilities among of the five mission areas by the means of operating jointly, using the same systems, doctrine and terminology."[42] However, this report does not indicate what entity is bringing all of this together. In addition to integrating operational management processes and procedures, the report indicated a need to educate, train and exercise all stakeholders on "incident management, the planning discipline, legal authorities, capabilities, and field-level crisis leadership."[43] This implies there is a lack of a common understanding of each organization's capabilities and limitations which creates a barrier that hinders the flow of information sharing between organizations.

In February 2010, Secretary Napolitano published the Department's first Quadrennial Homeland Security Review (QHSR) to align the Department of Homeland Security programs and activities with their partners under what is known as a "whole-of-government" approach towards national security.[44] The QHSR defines DHS's role as

---

[39] National Preparedness Goal, 1.

[40] U.S. Department of Homeland Security, *National Preparedness Report*, Government Printing Office (Washington, D.C., 2012), ii and iii.

[41] Ibid, ii.

[42] The Federal Response to Hurricane Katrina: Lessons Learned, 72.

[43] Ibid, 72-73.

[44] U.S. Department of Homeland Security, "Creation of the Department of Homeland Security," Department of Homeland Security, http://www.dhs.gov/creation-department-homeland-security (accessed October 8, 2012).

largely one of leadership among the Department of Justice, Department of Defense, Department of State, the Federal Bureau of Investigation, and the National Counterterrorism Center who also own critical capabilities in counterterrorism, defense, intelligence, and diplomacy needed to protect the Homeland. [45] As such, the Department of Homeland Security has no authority to task other organizations and is fully dependent on building capacity with other agencies to achieve its desired end states. A recent Government Accountability Office report review of the QHSR indicates a need for the Department "to expand joint operations and intelligence capabilities, including enhanced domain awareness."[46]

Today, the Department of Homeland Security capabilities are derived from its ability to build a unity of effort across the five mission areas. This is important because many of the Department's activities overlap missions and functions provided by other Federal departments and agencies. A current goal of the Department is "to enhance its intelligence, information sharing, and integrated operations by instituting a mechanism to integrate the Department of Homeland Security's intelligence elements, increasing operational capability and harmonizing operations with Federal, State, local, territorial, tribal, non-governmental, private sector, and international partners."[47]

Challenges of the Department of Homeland Security Organizational Structure

The Department of Homeland Security faces a number of challenges that are rooted within its broad mandate. Among these challenges is the Department's need to resolve its inter- and intra-agency conflicts between authorities, policies, and procedures;

---

[45] Quadrennial Homeland Security Review Report, iii.

[46] United States, Quadrennial Homeland Security Review: Enhanced Stakeholder Consultation and Use of Risk Information Could Strengthen Future Reviews, U.S. Government Accountability Office (GAO-11-873), Government Printing Office (Washington, D.C., 2011), 37.

[47] Department of Homeland Security Strategic Plan, Fiscal Years 2012-2016, 27.

and the need for the Department to design management systems that support management functions "to ensure [the] effective communication, coordination and integration of efforts across the Department."[48]

Conflict between Authorities, Policies and Procedures

A unified approach to addressing authorities, policies and procedures is a key factor in leading the efforts within the homeland security enterprise. In a report to Congress, the Government Accountability Office stated, "Given Department of Homeland Security's leadership responsibilities in homeland security, it is critical that its programs are operating as efficient and effectively as possible, are sustainable, and continue to mature to address pressing security needs."[49] In support of the Department of Homeland Security, there has been numerous laws enacted that expand, modify, or clarify Department's roles and responsibilities within the homeland security enterprise.[50] However, the duplication of effort in intelligence gathering, cyber security, strategic planning for national preparedness and the lack of information sharing continue to be an issue, because

> The Department of Homeland Security doesn't include all of the Federal government's major homeland security agencies [such as] the Department of State, Department of Defense, Department of Justice, and Department of Health and Human Services along with key agencies of our government [that] all play very important roles in protecting our homeland security.[51]

---

[48] Richard L. Draft, *Organization Theory and Design* (Mason, Ohio: South-Western Cengage Learning, 2008), 90.

[49] United States, Department of Homeland Security Progress Made and Work Remaining in Implementing Homeland Security Missions 10 Years After 9/11: Report to Congressional Requesters, U.S. Government Accountability Office (GAO-11-881), Government Printing Office (Washington, D.C., 2011), Summary.

[50] Ibid, 10.

[51] Senator Joseph I. Lieberman, Chairman, "Senator Joseph I. Lieberman holds a hearing on Homeland Security Department's Roles/Missions." *FDCH Political Transcripts (n.d.):* Military & Government Collection, EBSCOhost, 2, (accessed July 31, 2012).

For example, during Hurricane Katrina "many agencies took action under their own independent authorities while also responding to mission assignments from the FEMA, creating further process confusion and potential duplication of efforts."[52] Another example is the need for sharing national intelligence capabilities between the DHS, the Central Intelligence Agency, and the Federal Bureau of Investigation; since the CIA and FBI not are a part of the Department of Homeland Security, but critical to the homeland security enterprise. One more example as previously discussed is the authority given to the FEMA Director to bypass the Department's Secretary and gain direct access to the President in response to a domestic emergency.

A way to address authorities, policies and procedures is through negotiation and the development of a memorandum of understanding or a memorandum of agreement to promote collaboration and establish a formal partnership between departments and organizations. However, critics of these types of agreements believe that periodic review processes are too difficult to manage with personnel turnover. Today, the Department has published little, if any, literature on their current actions to resolve the conflicts between authorities, policies and procedures.

A Need to Integrate Internal Management Functions and Systems

From its conception, the Department of Homeland Security has faced a number of intra-Departmental management challenges associated with the integration of 22 dissimilar agencies and their specific resource requirements that cross multiple mission areas such as military, law enforcement, agriculture, biomedicine, disaster relief,

---

[52] The Federal Response to Hurricane Katrina: Lessons Learned, 52.

insurance, fire service, etc.[53] In Congressional testimony, former department Inspector General Richard Skinner stated, "When we stood up, the management support functions were shortchanged. We brought over all of the operational aspects of the 22 different agencies, but we did not bring the management support functions to support those operations. And as a result, we've been digging ourselves out of a hole ever since."[54] A 2005 Government Accountability Office report states, "Critical to meeting this challenge is the integration of DHS's varied management processes, systems and people - in such areas as information technology, financial management, procurement, and human capital - as well as administrative support."[55]

In response, the Department established the Business Transformation Office (BTO) beneath the Under Secretary for Management - a component agency - to serve as the day-to-day link between the Headquarters element and the various components to achieve its management integration efforts. The Department of Homeland Security defines their management integration efforts by three levels of activities.

> *Strategic Integration* - consists of efforts to ensure that component activities and acquisitions align with the Departments mission goals through appropriate leadership oversight and policies and procedures.[56]
>
> *Operational Coordination* – consists of the delivery of management services in order to increase cross-component collaboration and reduce costs by achieving efficiencies for managing assets such as real property, for procuring volume

---

[53] Kenneth C. Laudon, and Jane P. Laudon, *Management Information Systems: Managing the Digital Firm*, Ninth Edition (New Jersey: Pearson Prentice Hall, 2006), 41.

[54] Richard L. Skinner, Former Inspector General, U.S. Department of Homeland Security. "The Future of Homeland Security." *FDCH Congressional Testimony* (July 12, 2012): Military & Government Collection, EBSCOhost, 16, (accessed July 31, 2012).

[55] United States, Department of Homeland Security: A Comprehensive and Sustained Approach Needed to Achieve Management Integration: Report to Congressional Requesters, U.S. Government Accountability Office (GAO-05-139), Government Printing Office (Washington, D.C., 2005), Executive Summary.

[56] United States, *Department of Homeland Security: Actions Taken Toward Management Integration, but a Comprehensive Strategy Is Still Needed*, U.S. Government Accountability Office (GAO-10-131), Government Printing Office (Washington, D.C., 2009), 6.

discounts of supplies and services, and acquiring common technology platforms through shared information technology infrastructure.[57]

Functional Integration - consists of management oversight of component-level internal controls and standard operating policies to ensure department wide compliance with presidential directives, congressional mandates, and other legal requirements and DHS policies; and consistent business practices that support financial reporting and operational assurance statements.[58]

The Business Transformation Office consisting of a director with four additional staff was established because the Department does not have a strong and stable mid-level management structure between the Headquarters element and its 22 component agencies. Ideally, the Business Transformation Office would monitor functional integration efforts and communicate management initiatives across the department.[59] However, the Under Secretary for Management did not have the authority to hold the component's heads "accountable for implementing management integration through reporting relationships."[60] A 2009 Government Accountability Office report indicated that over this time period the Department stopped working to develop a comprehensive strategy for this integration of efforts as outlined in a prior 2005 Government Accountability Office report.[61] Instead the Department focused its efforts on building operational coordination rather than strategic and functional integration. As such, the different levels of information requirements are not being met.

Exacerbating this challenge is the lack of common information systems to support seamless data collection and storage. An information system is defined as "a set of interrelated components that collect (or retrieve), process, store, and distribute

---

[57] Ibid.

[58] Ibid.

[59] Department of Homeland Security: A Comprehensive and Sustained Approach Needed to Achieve Management Integration: Report to Congressional Requesters, 17.

[60] Department of Homeland Security: Actions Taken Toward Management Integration, but a Comprehensive Strategy Is Still Needed, Executive Summary.

[61] Ibid.

information to support decision making and control in an organization."[62] Initially, manual data calls served as the primary means the Department of Homeland Security used for providing senior leadership with integrated information.[63] As resources became available, the Department's information systems evolved to enable a common data collection and storage system to disseminate information across the Department and among its interagency partners. This is important because the lack of a common information system can affect decision-making, coordination and control in the organization.[64] Over time, the Department of Homeland Security has made progress towards consolidating numerous component systems to improve collective efforts to resolve problems with human capital, resource management and information sharing.[65] Still "after nearly a decade, the Department of Homeland Security's failure to integrate its management practices remains on the GAO's High Risk list."[66] A current goal of the Department is "to improve the cross-developmental management, policy, and functional integration by enhancing and integrating Departmental management functions."[67] Three critical management challenges that must be addressed reside in the areas of resource management, acquisition oversight and workforce morale.

Department of Homeland Security Resource Management

The Department of Homeland Security must prepare to effectively counter natural and man-made hazards that pose a threat to the nation. Effective preparation requires

---

[62] Laudon and Laudon, Management Information Systems, 13.

[63] U.S. Department of Homeland Security, "Written testimony of DHS Management Under Secretary Rafael Borras for a House Committee on Homeland Security, Subcommittee on Oversight, Investigations, and Management hearing titled 'Building One DHS: Why Can't Management Information be Integrated'," Department of Homeland Security, http://www.dhs.gov/news/2012/02/29/written-testimony-dhs-management-under-secretary-house-homeland-security (accessed September 7, 2012).

[64] Laudon and Laudon, Management Information Systems, 13.

[65] "Building One DHS."

[66] Ibid.

[67] Department of Homeland Security Strategic Plan, Fiscal Years 2012-2016, 24.

every component of the department to integrate its planning, resourcing, doctrine, technology development and fielding, training and exercise, and manning requirements under a single management system. As such, the Department adopted an approach -- similar to the Department of Defense -- establishing the Planning, Programming, Budgeting and Execution (PPBE) management system to gain Congressional approval for authorizations and appropriations. The PPBE process is an integrated business process designed to align resources with capability gaps with the intent of minimizing a duplication of effort.[68] In recent testimony Senator Lieberman stated, "The department's operational components, I think are still not adequately integrated with its headquarters and with each other. And that causes problems. That causes at least less than optimal use of the department's resources,"[69] such as, "setting requirements and effectively carrying them out for major acquisitions and ensuring that these acquisition programs stay on track while they're under way."[70] This is important because the competition for resources is challenging. For example, imagine managing the acquisition of U.S. Coast Guard's air assets with the same resource budget of the air assets of Office of Air and Marine Interdiction within Customs and Border Protection. Regarding aircraft, Custom and Border Protection relies on manned and unmanned aircraft to enforce "security at and between ports of entry along the border"[71]; while, the U.S. Coast Guard relies on both manned long-range fixed wing aircraft and helicopters to enforce "security of U.S. ports,

---

[68] U.S. Department of Homeland Security, *Capital Planning and Investment Control Guide: Version 4.0*, The Office of the Chief Information Officer, Government Printing Office (Washington, D.C., 2007), 4.

[69] Lieberman, "Senator Joseph I. Lieberman", 3.

[70] Ibid.

[71] Congressional Research Service, Department of Homeland Security FY2013 Appropriations, by the Congressional Research Service, October 2012 (Washington, D.C.: Government Printing Office, 2012), 41.

coastal and inland waterways, and territorial waters"[72] which is not achievable under the same acquisition budget due to differing personnel, technology and maintenance requirements. As a result, resource allocation, acquisition and investment serve as friction points between the components and leads to a competition for resources. The management framework needed to prioritize strategic requirements remains immature. A current goal of the Department is "to improve the cross-developmental management, policy, and functional integration by strengthening the integrated investment life cycle and acquisition oversight and increasing analytic capability and capacity."[73]

Duplication of Oversight within the Department of Homeland Security

Based the powers given to Congress through the Constitution, its roles in National Security include the oversight of activities within the Department of Homeland Security. Congressional oversight of the Department of Homeland Security is provided by 86 committees and subcommittees split between the U.S. House of Representatives and the U.S. Senate.[74] In order to influence how Congress discharges these Constitutional responsibilities, the Department of Homeland Security must have an effective ability to respond on resourcing matters. Likewise the duplication of oversight between the Department of Homeland Security and its components has been a significant issue since its conception. For example, a recent Government Accountability Office report stated,

> The Department of Homeland Security (DHS) does not know the total amount its components invest in research and development (R&D) and does not have policies and guidance for defining R&D and overseeing R&D resources across the department. As a result, it is difficult for DHS to oversee components' R&D efforts and align them with agency wide R&D goals and priorities. Developing specific policies and guidance could assist DHS components in better understanding how to report R&D activities, and better position DHS to

---

[72] Ibid, 55.

[73] Department of Homeland Security Strategic Plan, Fiscal Years 2012-2016, 24.

[74] Author's notes from a slide presentation by a Department of Homeland Security representative on March 13, 2013.

determine how much the agency invests in R&D to effectively oversee these investments.[75]

In Congressional testimony, Admiral (Retired) Thad W. Allen stated, "The most robust command and control functions and capabilities in the Department reside at the component level with the National Operation Center serving as a collator of information and reporting to the Secretary."[76] This is a significant issue for dedicating and organizing resources, managing information and producing a common operating picture, and making decisions and taking action. A way to address the duplication of oversight between the DHS and its components is by establishing a central body to oversee the integration of processes and procedures within the Department. Today, the Department has published little, if any, literature on their current actions to resolve the duplication of oversight between DHS and its components.

Cultural and Morale issues plaguing Department of Homeland Security

From the outset, "the Department of Homeland Security continues to have workforce moral challenges as reflected in the annual ratings done in the Federal Human Capital Survey. These have improved over the years, but nowhere near to the extent needed."[77] In January 2007, the *Homeland Security Advisory Council's Homeland Security Cultural Task Force* proposed six recommendations designed to assist Secretary Chertoff with improving "the Department's leaders in creating and sustaining an

---

[75] United States, *Department of Homeland Security: Oversight and Coordination of Research and Development Should Be Strengthened,* U.S. Government Accountability Office (GAO-12-837), Government Printing Office (Washington, D.C., 2012), 2.

[76] Thad W. Allen, Admiral (Retired) United States Coast Guard, "The Future of Homeland Security," *FDCH Congressional Testimony* (July 12, 2012): Military & Government Collection, EBSCOhost, 3, (accessed July 31, 2012).

[77] Lieberman, "Senator Joseph I. Lieberman", 3.

energetic, dedicated, and empowering mission-focused organization."[78] The Cultural

Task Force recommendations were:

(a) *DHS Headquarters must further define and crystallize its role and relationship to its component organizations* through building trust by the means of empowerment of not only the components, but also the empowerment of its employees.
(b) *Implement Homeland Security Management and Leadership Models:* A proposed set of expectations of Involvement, Inspiration, Innovation and Service.
(c) *Establish an Operational Leadership Position:* The creation of a Deputy Secretary for Operations responsible for generating and sustaining seamless operational integration and alignment of the component organizations.
(d) *Create leadership empowered teamwork and a "Blended Culture"*: The appointment of a senior career employee to support the Secretary in the continuous development and sustainment of the overarching/blended culture within the Department.
(e) *Engage the State, Local, Tribal and Private Sector in an "Outside the Beltway-Focused" Collaborative Process.*
(f) *Institutionalize the Opportunity for Innovation*: The appointment of an innovation official responsible for tracking the Department's actions on ideas from their initial delivery to their implementation, modification, or rejection - and then providing formal feedback to the submitter on the rationale for the Department's actions. [79]

However, in the conclusion of this report, the Cultural Task Force acknowledged

that even after implementing these recommendations, the integration of 22 separate

organizations into an efficient and effective department is a most daunting task because

"culture is about people, relationships and inspirations, and how the people of the

department view its leadership, the organization itself and its purpose, and the importance

of one's individual role within the department."[80] In 2009, the Department of Homeland

Security began a second attempt to address its culture and morale issues through the use

of multiple documents such as the 2010 *Quadrennial Homeland Security Review*, a

---

[78] U.S. Department of Homeland Security, *Report of the Homeland Security Culture Task Force*, Government Printing Office (Washington D.C., 2007), 1.

[79] Ibid, 1,3,5-8.

[80] Brittany Ballenstedt, "Task Force recommends measures to improve DHS culture," *Government Executive*, February 13, 2007, under "Management," http://www.govexec.com/management/2007/02/task-force-recommends-measures-to-improve-dhs-culture/23725/ (accessed August 3, 2012).

Bottom-Up Review and the *Secretary's Efficiency Review* with the aim "promoting greater accountability, and customer satisfaction" [81] within the organization. A 2011 Federal Employee Viewpoint Survey clearly indicates culture and morale issues still exist within the Department in the areas of Leadership and Knowledge Management, Results-Oriented Performance Culture, Talent Management, and Job Satisfaction, which all score lower than other federal departments and agencies.[82] A current goal of the Department is to enhance the DHS workforce by strengthening coordination with DHS through cross-Departmental training and career paths; improving employee health, wellness, and resilience; increasing workforce diversity; and, reducing reliance on contractors.[83]

Summary

A review of the literature has revealed three critical issues that need to be addressed by the Department of Homeland Security. First, the Department needs to determine a way to integrate its internal resources management activities. Secondly, the Department needs to enhance its culture so its workforce can perform more efficiently and effectively. Finally, the Department needs to improve the way it integrates (coordinate, communicate and collaborate) it capabilities with other stakeholders throughout the homeland security enterprise. A summary of the Department's future goals suggest this can be accomplished by: improving cross-department management, policy, and functional integration; enhancing its intelligence, information sharing and integrated operations; and, enhancing the DHS workforce by "[building] human resource

---

[81] Department of Homeland Security Strategic Plan, Fiscal Years 2012-2016, 23.
[82] U.S. Department of Homeland Security, *2011 Federal Employee Viewpoint Survey: Empowering Employees*, U.S. Office of Personnel Management, Government Printing Office (Washington D.C., 2011), 12.
[83] Department of Homeland Security Strategic Plan, Fiscal Years 2012-2016, 24.

programs that support Departmental missions and goals"[84] to improve its culture and morale issues. However, further study is required to determine ways to: de-conflict the overlap of authorities, policies, and procedures between departments and agencies; resolve the duplication of Congressional oversight provided by 86 committees and subcommittees; and most important, address U.S. public expectations of their government during crisis.

The next chapter will analyze the Department of Homeland Security's internal management systems, specifically those that impact organizational functions such as vision, teamwork, values and information, and demonstrate the benefits of creating an integrating element within the Department.

---

[84] Ibid, 25.

CHAPTER 3: SYNCHRONING INTERNAL MANAGEMENT SYSTEMS

Overview

The Department of Homeland Security is a large, complex organization that is responsible for executing a variety of missions and serving a broad range of stakeholders.[1] Effective execution of these missions often requires the expertise and capabilities of multiple Departmental components. Achieving mission success requires internal coordination and communication among 22 different management systems ranging from military and law enforcement to biomedicine and disaster relief. The accountability for management functions resides with each of the component heads.[2] Currently, no single office or component has been charged with the responsibility to ensure management functions are integrated across the Department. Each component is continuing to function under its separate organizational culture and structure based on differing resource requirements and conflicting processes. An effective management system is one which integrates all of the common management functions into one coherent system to gain efficiencies and cost-effectiveness. By examining the management functions of the Joint Staff, the Department of Homeland Security can learn ways to integrate its 22 different management systems. There are several benefits for combining the Department's management systems including: streamlining management functions; synchronizing planning and resource management; reducing the duplication of oversight; and, maturing the organization. This chapter will investigate each one of these four benefits in more detail by applying the Department of Defense hierarchy and the

---

[1] U.S. Department of Homeland Security, *Homeland Security Risk Management Doctrine: Risk Management Fundamentals*, Government Printing Office (Washington D.C., 2011), 1.

[2] Thad W. Allen, Admiral (Retired) United States Coast Guard, "The Future of Homeland Security," *FDCH Congressional Testimony* (July 12, 2012): Military & Government Collection, EBSCOhost, 2, (accessed July 31, 2012).

Joint Staff functions to demonstrate how creating an intermediate management element will serve as a cornerstone for integration within the Department of Homeland Security.

Streamlining Management Functions

The capacity of the Department of Homeland Security to operate as a cohesive organization is affected by the failure of its internal management practices. "In order to meet and overcome current and future threats," Senator Susan M. Collins, R-Maine, told a Senate Homeland Security committee, "the Department of Homeland Security must support its components with stronger management."[3] This is important because the effective integration of management functions will reduce the Department's exposure to risk.

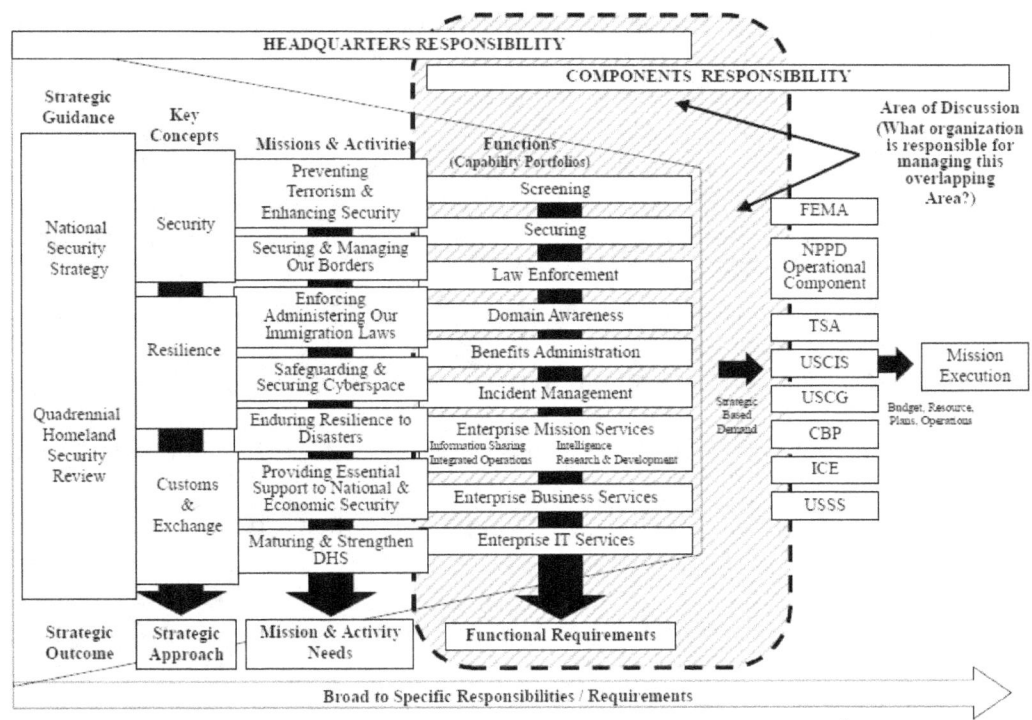

Figure 4. DHS Integrated Strategic Framework.[4]

[3] Susan M. Collins, Ranking Member, Senate Homeland Security and Governmental Affairs, Committee, "The Future of Homeland Security," *FDCH Congressional Testimony* (July 12, 2012): Military & Government Collection, EBSCOhost, 5, (accessed July 31, 2012).

[4] U.S. Department of Homeland Security, *Department of Homeland Security Strategic Plan, Fiscal Years 2012-2016*, Government Printing Office (Washington, D.C., 2012), A-3.

Figure 4 illustrates the Department of Homeland Security's integrated strategic framework which links strategy to tasks. This chart describes how the Department links its goals and objectives from the *Quadrennial Homeland Security Review* to the mission execution requirements of its components.[5] Each mission and activity interrelates with various capabilities found among the 22 component agencies which it turn needs to be integrated to achieve efficiencies prior to being given to a component to execute their given mission. In figure 4, the author's discussion primarily focuses on what "entity" within the Department is integrating the management functions and requirements within the encircled area because the capability portfolios fall within a gray area of responsibility between the headquarters and the components.

According to Professor Keith Laudon, author of *Management Information Systems*, "organizations can be divided into strategic, management and operational levels"[6] and common functional areas. The four most common functional areas found within the Department's headquarters and its components are: information sharing and intelligence; operations, planning, training and exercising; resource development and procurement; and, human resources requirements. The premise of Laudon's model suggests that "information systems serve each of these levels and functions."[7] Figure 5 provides a visual depiction of Laudon's model applied to the current Department of Homeland Security hierarchy.

---

[5] Ibid.

[6] Kenneth C. Laudon, and Jane P. Laudon, *Management Information Systems: Managing the Digital Firm*, Ninth Edition (New Jersey: Pearson Prentice Hall, 2006), 41.

[7] Ibid.

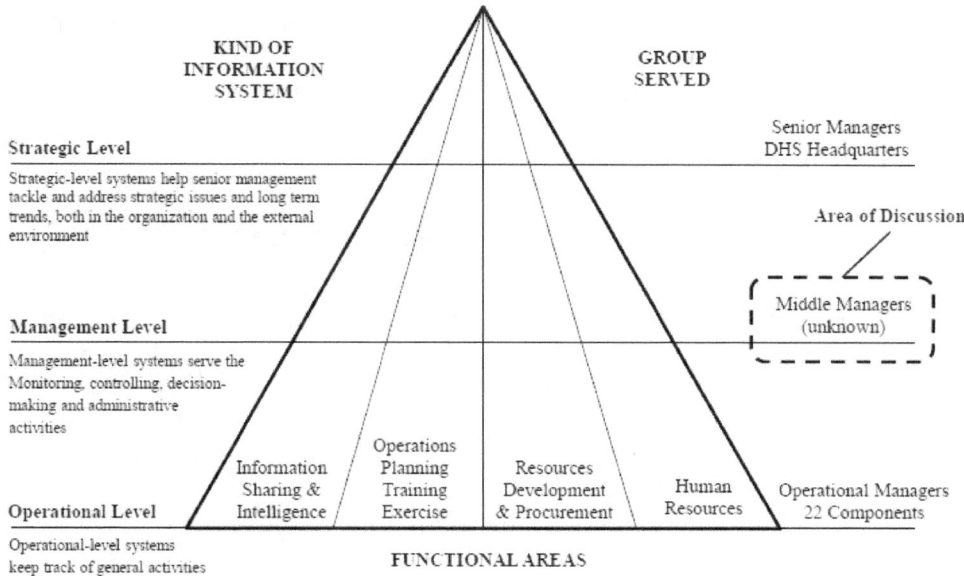

Figure 5. Information System within DHS.[8]

The figure shows a pyramid divided into three hierarchical management levels with the

four common functional areas listed along the bottom. Viewing the Department of

Homeland Security hierarchy using Laudon's model brings into question what

organization or component serves the mid-level management function.

To illustrate Laudon's model within the Department of Defense, the Joint Staff

serves as the middle-level management responsible for assisting the Chairman of the

Joint Chiefs of Staff with providing the Department with "unified strategic direction of

the combatant forces; unified operation of the combatant commands; and the integration

of land, naval, and air forces."[9] Each of the Joint Staff directorates is responsible for

working together to provide a day-to-day link between the Office of the Secretary of

Defense and the Service components. The synergy created by the Joint Staff

management functions helps strengthen the Department and serves as a means to achieve

a unity of effort. Creating a mid-level management structure within the Department of

---

[8] The author's illustration of Laudon's model applied to DHS heirarchy.

[9] U.S. Joint Chiefs of Staff, "Director Responsibility Statement," Joint Chiefs of Staff, http://www.jcs.mil/page.aspx?id=13 (accessed March 10, 2013).

Homeland Security, which can integrate functional requirements and administrative activities, would clearly create a strong and sustainable foundation for building a unity of effort among its component agencies.

Synchronizing Resource Management

Capability development is dependent on the budget. A current goal of the Department is to improve its cross-developmental management, policy, and functional integration by strengthening its integrated life cycle investment process and its acquisition oversight program "to enable cross-component budget analysis and decision support"[10] for input to its Analytic Agenda.[11] This is especially important considering size of the Department of Homeland Security budget in comparison to the Department of Defense. The much smaller funding stream "cries" for greater coordination and "jointness" than the Department of Defense. Aligning Departmental resources to operational requirements in a collaborative effort allows leaders to make decisions to drive technology investments and acquisition in an efficient and effective manner. Unfortunately, the largest prevention and response components[12] dominate the resource requirements within the Department. Figure 6 illustrates the Department of Homeland Security's Integrated Investment Life Cycle Model in relation to its PPBE system.

---

[10] Department of Homeland Security Strategic Plan, Fiscal Years 2012-2016, 24.

[11] The DHS Analytic Agenda is a senior leadership tool to help shape planning and budgets.

[12] U.S. Customs and Border Protection, U.S. Coast Guard, FEMA, Transportation Security Adminstration, and U.S. Immigration & Customs Enforcement account for nearly 80% of the Department of Homeland Security's budget.

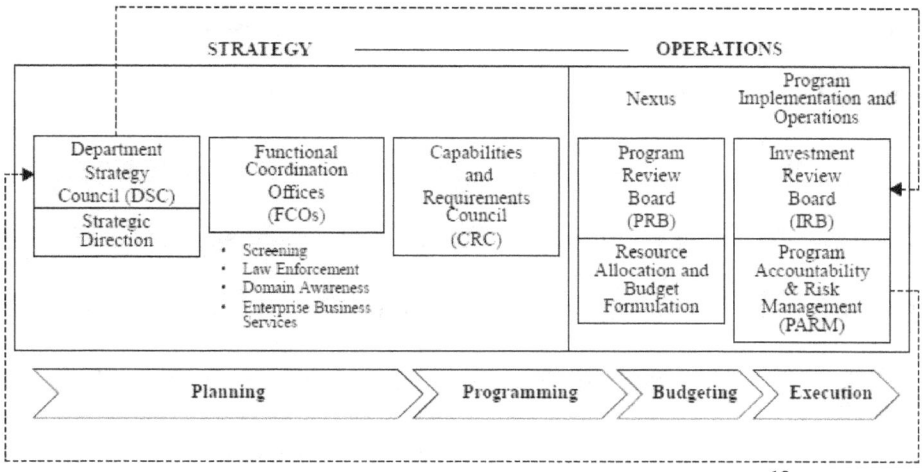

Figure 6. DHS Integrated Investment Life Cycle Model.[13]

The primary components responsible for managing the PPBE process are the Office of Policy and the Office of Management. Whereas, each Functional Coordination Office is responsible for developing an independent assessment of its capability needs to be reviewed by the *Capabilities and Requirements Council* for further analysis and integration. [14] A recent Government Accountability Office report states that, the "Department of Homeland Security does not yet have enough skilled personnel in various areas, such as acquisition management; and, has not yet developed an integrated financial management system, impacting its ability to have ready access to reliable information for informed decision-making." [15] For the Department of Homeland Security to mature and build a unity of effort among its components, it must recruit and retain skilled civil service and contract personnel and integrate its components' personnel, similar to the Joint Staff, to develop and help guide the PPBE process across the Department.

---

[13] Department of Homeland Security Strategic Plan, Fiscal Years 2012-2016, A-2.

[14] Ibid.

[15] Diane Barnes, "Organizational Problems Persist at DHS: Auditors," *Global Security Newswire*, September 8, 2011, under "Daily News on Nuclear, Biological & Chemical Weapons, Terrorism and Related Issues," http://www.nti.org/gsn/article/organizational-problems-persist-at-dhs-auditors/ (accessed August 6, 2012).

As previously mentioned, the Department of Homeland Security did adopt the Department of Defense Planning, Programing and Budgeting and Execution System (PPBES) as their means to equitably deliver its components' resource requirements. Within DoD, the PPBES is the primary resource management system designed to link strategy, programs, and resources by identifying the size, structure, and equipment for the future force. This process is similar in many ways to a corporate or family budget building process. The Services are responsible for their respective budgets, captured in the development of the Program Objectives Memorandum (POM),[16] which then feeds the Secretary of Defense's budget submission to the President. Within the Joint Staff, the Joint Staff J8 Directorate for Force Structure Resources and Assessment serves as the integrator between the Office of the Secretary of Defense and the Service components for many of the functions within PPBES including: capability assessments, the integrated priority list, and issue nomination during the program and budget review process. Success within the PPBES requires experienced personnel from within each of the Service components to help identify issues and bring them to the forefront. The personnel structure needed to assist with the Service POMs build are assigned to the Joint Staff J8 on a permanent basis. In the same manner, for the Department of Homeland Security to allocate resources more effectively requires a permanent staff of skilled professionals from each functional area capable of providing a joint perspective on strategic decision making, resource prioritization, and program execution.

---

[16] A Program Objectives Memorandum is a recommendation of the DOD components [Services and defense agencies] to the SECDEF on the allocation of resources for proposed programs to achieve assigned missions and objectives. Proposed programs are consistent with the strategy and guidance stated in the Defense Planning Guidance and constrained by Fiscal Guidance from U.S. Joint Chiefs of Staff Instruction, *Chairman of The Joint Chiefs Of Staff, Combatant Commanders, Chief, National Guard Bureau, And Joint Staff Participation in the Planning, Programming, Budgeting And Execution Process,* CJCSI 8501.01B, Washington DC: Joint Chiefs of Staff, August 21, 2012, Enclosure B.

Reducing Duplication of Oversight within Department of Homeland Security

A recent Government Accountability Office report notes the inconsistencies in which the Department integrates its oversight procedures.[17] A duplication of oversight occurs when different components independently collect and store the same piece of information. These shortcomings "have contributed to schedule delays, cost increases, and performance problems in a number of programs aimed at delivering important mission capabilities, such as a system to detect certain nuclear materials in vehicles and containers at ports."[18] This is a significant issue for dedicating and organizing resources, managing information and producing a common operating picture, making decisions and taking action. The Department of Homeland Security can address these shortcomings by combining some of the smaller component agencies with similar functions under a common directorate to streamline operations and become more efficient. For example, the author would merge the management, intelligence and analysis, operations and plans, and resource development and assessment directorates under one directorate. The potential benefit to the Department alone would save several billion dollars through the elimination of redundant positions, the establishment of common processes, and the sharing of common systems.

Maturing the Department of Homeland Security

Linking Vision with Departmental Values

The Secretary of Homeland Security Janet Napolitano published the current Department's strategic vision statement in the 2010 *Quadrennial Homeland Security Review Report*. It reads, "The vision of homeland security is to ensure a homeland that is

---

[17] Barnes, "Organizational Problems Persist."
[18] Ibid.

safe, secure, and resilient against terrorism and other hazards where American interests, aspirations, and way of life can thrive."[19] This vision statement provides the Department with a roadmap which links the current operational environment consisting of threats from terrorism, cyber-attacks, pandemics, and catastrophic natural disasters to the desired end state of achieving a safe, prosperous, and secure Nation. Over the next few months, Secretary Napolitano will reveal her new vision for the evolution of the Department from what she calls DHS 2.0[20] to DHS 3.0 which places emphasis on engagement and integration.[21] Arthur A. Thompson Jr., author of *Crafting and Executing Strategy: The Quest for Competitive Advantage* suggests the strategic vision should be linked to the organization's core values. Values directly relate to the organizations treatment of employees and customers, its integrity, ethics, innovation, and social responsibility.[22] The Department of Homeland Security has embraced five overarching core values: Duty - "Embodying Integrity, Responsibility, and Accountability"; Respect - "Honoring Our Partners and One Another"; Innovation - "Creating Opportunities"; and, Vigilance - "Safeguarding America."[23] Only Respect and Vigilance have been in place since the Department defined its core values in 2004.[24] Figure 7 compares the Department of Homeland Security core values with its major component agencies.

---

[19] U.S. Department of Homeland Security, *Quadrennial Homeland Security Review Report*, Government Printing Office (Washington, D.C., 2010), 3.

[20] DHS 2.0 focuses the Department's efforts on building stronger partnerships with Federal, State, local, tribal governments and the private and non-government sectors.

[21] U.S. Department of Homeland Security, "Secretary of Homeland Security Janet Napolitano's Third Annual Address on the State of Homeland Security," Department of Homeland Security, http://www.dhs.gov/news/2013/02/26/secretary-homeland-security-janet-napolitano%E2%80%99s-third-annual-address-state-homeland (accessed March 16, 2013).

[22] Arthur A. Thompson Jr., A.J. Strickland III, and John E. Gamble, *Crafting and Executing Strategy: The Quest for Competitive Advantage* (Boston: McGraw-Hill, 2005), 21.

[23] U.S. Department of Homeland Security, *Department of Homeland Security Strategic Plan, Fiscal Years 2008-2013*, Government Printing Office (Washington, D.C., 2008), 3.

[24] Ibid, 5.

DUTY, INTEGRITY, RESPECT, VIGILANCE, & INNOVATION								
Department of Homeland Security	DHS HQ	TSA	USCG	FEMA	CBP	ICE	USSS	USCIS
Duty	X	X	X	X	X	X	X	X
Integrity	X	X	X	X	X	X	X	X
Respect	X			X				X
Vigilance	X				X			X
Innovation	X	X	X					
Team Spirit		X	X					
Greater Good of the Coast Guard			X					
Personal Initiative			X					
Drive for Success			X					
Compassion				X				
Fairness				X				
Service to Country					X			
Courage						X	X	
Excellence						X		
Justice							X	
Honesty							X	
Loyalty							X	
Ingenuity								X

Figure 7. Department of Homeland Security Core Values by Major Component Agency.[25]

This figure shows a broad array of core values embraced by the headquarters and its major components agencies. Of the 18 core values listed above, only Duty and Integrity are commonly shared among the major component agencies. This spreadsheet does not account for the wide array of core values found within the 15 smaller agencies which will cause this list to significantly grow beyond what is currently depicted. According to Thompson, an organization's core values are defined as "the beliefs, business principles, and practices that guide the conduct of its business, pursuit of its strategic vision, and the behavior of organizational personnel."[26] Values are important because DHS is frequently criticized for its failure to come together as a cohesive organization. Too many core values dilute the Department's business principles that serve as a common bond that influence employee and customer expectations. For example, when DHS hires a new employee, what mechanism is the Department going to use to instill duty, integrity, respect, vigilance, and innovation within its workforce in order to retain their talent over

---

[25] The author's spreadsheet depicts the broad array of core values found within DHS headquarters and its seven major component agencies.

[26] Thompson, Strickland, and Gamble, *Crafting And Executing Strategy*, 21.

time. By establishing a joint system for training and education is a way DHS can link its vision with Departmental values for attracting and developing a corps of career professionals. Upon analyzing Figure 7, there is an opportunity for the Department and its components to reexamine their five overarching core values, in an approach similar to the Department of Defense, and better connect them to the Secretary's vision of DHS 3.0 and its future workforce.

In 2009, the Department of Defense commissioned a research study to assist in defining the Department's core values and how it linked to the vision of the future workforce. The research group took into consideration the five Services core values and the professional needs of the civilian workforce prior to developing the Department's core values.

LEADERSHIP, PROFESSIONALISM, & TECHNICAL KNOW-HOW						
Department of Defense	DoD/OSD	USAF	USA	USMC	USN	USCG
Duty	X		X			X
Integrity	X	X	X			X
Honor	X		X	X	X	X
Courage	X		X	X	X	
Loyalty	X		X			
Service Before Self/Greater Good of the Coast Guard	X	X	X			X
Excellence in all we do		X				
Respect			X			
Commitment				X	X	
Innovation						X
Team Spirit						X
Personal Initiative						X
Drive for Success						X

Figure 8. Department of Defense Core Values by Service Component. [27]

Figure 8 compares the Department of Defense's core values by Service component. The Department of Defense overarching core values are leadership, professionalism, and technical know-how which clearly conveys a message of full partnership between the military and civilians within the Department. For example, when DoD hires a new

---

[27] The author's spreadsheet depicts the broad array of core values found within DoD headquarters and its five service components.

42

employee (whether military or civilian), the Department instills within him or her the leadership, professional development, and technical training to be successful within the organization. Additionally, DoD placed special emphasis on identifying those core values that bond its uniform personnel together, which are: duty, integrity, ethics, honor, courage and loyalty.[28] The core value "ethics" was replaced with Selfless-Service at the conclusion of the 2009 study.[29] These core values build upon "the common ground shared by all individuals in each of the Services"[30] to help guide day-to-day interaction within the Department. In order for the Department of Homeland Security to mature, it must create a shared identity among its components by forming a common staff of skilled professionals capable of providing a joint perspective on strategic decision making, resource prioritization, and program execution.

Leadership and Organizational Culture

According to Edgar H. Schein, author of *Organizational Culture and Leadership*, "culture and leadership are two sides of the same coin in that leaders must first create cultures when they create groups and organizations."[31] Culture is defined as the set of values, norms, guiding beliefs, and understandings that is shared by members of an organization and taught to new members as the correct way to think, feel, and behave.[32] Every component within the Department of Homeland Security has its own internal leadership structure and culture. One factor influencing the Department's culture is the

---

[28] Military Leadership Diversity Commission, *Defense Core Values,* Military Leadership Diversity Commission Issue Paper 6 (Arlington, VA, 2009), 1.

[29] U.S. Joint Chiefs of Staff, *America's Military-Professions of Arms White Paper*, Joint Chiefs of Staff, Government Printing Office (Washington, D.C., 2012), 5.

[30] Military Leadership Diversity Commission, *Defense Core Values*, 1.

[31] Edgar H. Schein, *Organizational Culture and Leadership* (San Francisco: Jossey-Bass, 1992), 15.

[32] Richard L. Draft, *Organization Theory and Design* (Mason, Ohio: South-Western Cengage Learning, 2008), 374.

demography of the workforce. For example, a majority of the headquarters workforce is made up of retirees from other departments or agencies. As such, these retirees bring their own skills, experience, ethics, values, and prior organizational cultures to DHS. In addition to retirees, recent college graduates make up another portion of the headquarters workforce bringing their own skills, experience, ethics, and values to the Department. The combination of these subcultures creates a challenge for leadership in developing a shared understanding of Departmental goals, language, and procedures for solving problems. This is different from any large organization because DHS lacks the common culture needed to bring together these work forces, identify problems, examine possible actions, and make decisions. For the Department of Homeland Security to mature and unify its components, its leadership and management must find a way to build its organizational culture and influence the morale of its employees. For the Department of Homeland Security to operate more effectively requires the meshing of multiple subcultures interconnected by the development of a common education system similar to that of the Department of Defense's Joint Qualification System (JQS).

> The objective of the [DoD] JQS is to ensure a systematic, progressive, career-long development of officers in joint matters and to ensure that officers have the requisite experience and education to be highly proficient in joint matters, as directed in Title 10, USC, Chapter 38.[33]

The expected outcome of the JQS is to provide the joint force commander with trained, educated, and experienced officers who are capable of achieving unified action among "multiple military forces in operations conducted across domains such as land, sea, or air, in space, or in the information environment."[34] A product of the JQS is a skill designator

---

[33] U.S. Joint Chiefs of Staff Instruction, *Joint Officer Management Program Procedures,* CJCSI 1330.05 (Washington DC: Joint Chiefs of Staff, May 1, 2008), B-1.
[34] U.S. Joint Chiefs of Staff Instruction, *Joint Officer Management Program Procedures,* CJCSI 1330.05 (Washington DC: Joint Chiefs of Staff, May 1, 2008), B-2.

of a Joint Qualified Officer. Joint Qualified Officer's blend the analytical skills needed to carry out joint planning, training, exercising, and operations as part of a unified effort. In addition, a Joint Qualified Officer is groomed to take on a greater scope of responsibility at both the strategic and operational management levels. In a similar fashion, within the Department of Homeland Security, the introduction of a Homeland Security Professional would be one approach to developing a shared understanding of Departmental goals, language, and procedures for solving problems among its workforce. To be effective, the Homeland Security Professional requires specialized knowledge and skills that can only be obtained through formal training. A primary benefit of a Homeland Security Professional is to serve as a mentor for fostering shared concepts, ideas, and understanding among the 22 separate component agencies. Over time these Homeland Security Professionals will create a pool of skilled "DHS minded" leaders within the Department.

For an organization to be successful it must effectively manage its culture. Success will depend upon the organization's leadership gaining an understanding "of where there are potential incompatibilities with the culture of other organizations."[35] Whereas the Department of Defense thinks in four Service cultures, the organizational cultures and tensions between the "22 disparate organizations" in DHS are potentially more competitive than DoD. Within the DoD, there are significant cultural differences between the Service components that "reflect their assigned roles and missions, and the principal domain in which they operate."[36] Service culture is displayed on a daily basis by the wear of uniforms, rank and insignia, and service jargon. Similarly, Service culture

---

[35] Schein, Organizational Culture and Leadership, 384.
[36] U.S. Joint Chiefs of Staff, *America's Military*, 5.

is learned as a result of shared experiences such as basic training, customs and courtesies, the work environment, and is even passed down from generation to generation within a family. On the Joint Staff, culture is derived by leveraging unique expertise and competencies of the Service cultures. The strength from diversity of working together in a common environment over time fosters trust and confidence between the Service components and promotes mutual respect and cohesion to achieve a unity of effort within the Department.[37] In order to enable the Department of Homeland Security to mature requires its leadership to establish a common environment that focuses on problem-solving across internal boundaries which over time will foster trust and confidence among its components.

Summary

The chapter offered insight into why "the Department of Homeland Security must support its components with stronger management"[38] primarily for three reasons. First, the Department of Homeland Security has two levels of management which include: the Department's Headquarters leadership, management and personnel at the strategic level and the 22 component's leadership, management and personnel at the operational level. As such, both the Department headquarters and its components share the responsibility for integrating certain management systems within the Department. As a result, the Department has created a grey area within its internal management systems which allows random responsibility to occur for the integration of Departmental efforts. Figure 9 provides a depiction of this area of responsibility.

---

[37] Ibid.
[38] Collins, "Future of Homeland Security."

46

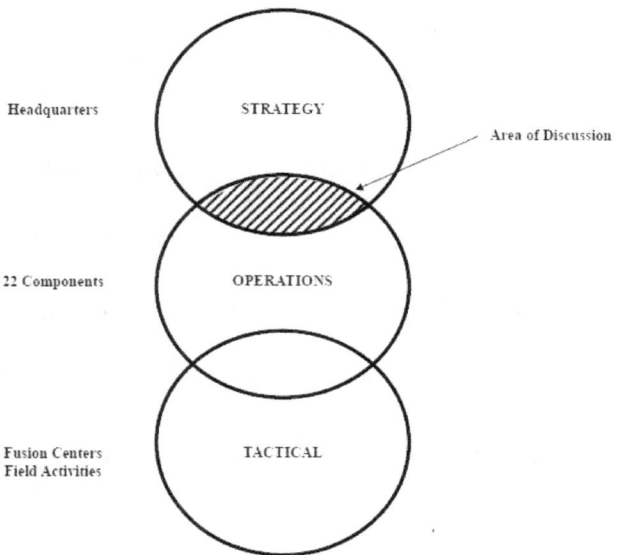

Figure 9. DHS Hierarchical Relationship.[39]

It shows three overlapping circles that represent the DHS hierarchical relationships and one overlapping greyed area that depicts the area of discussion. For the Department of Homeland Security to provide its component's with stronger management, it must leverage this grey area to facilitate better communication within the Department.

Secondly, each component is responsible for developing an independent assessment of their own capability, which in turn is reviewed by a specially formed mid-level *Capabilities and Requirements Council* for analysis and integration. To be more effective, the Department should establish a permanent mid-level management structure to integrate the common functional areas found within the headquarters and its components. For this new structure to be successful requires experienced personnel from within each of the Service components to be assigned on a three to five year rotational basis to help identify issues and bring them to the forefront.

---

[39] The author's depiction of the area of responsibility within the DHS hierarchical relationship that needs to addressed to provide the 22 component agencies with stronger management.

Third, the Department of Homeland Security can address its oversight shortcomings by combining some of the smaller component agencies with similar functions under a common directorate to streamline operations and become more efficient. Working together in a common environment fosters trust and confidence between the components and promotes mutual respect and cohesion to achieve a unity of effort within the Department.[40] Over time, this strength from diversity allows for establishment of common systems where people buy into this new culture to become more professional.

Finally, the Department of Homeland Security should revisit its five overarching core values and better connect them to the Secretary's vision of the future workforce. In order for the Department of Homeland Security to mature, it must create a shared identify among its components by forming a common staff of Homeland Security Professional capable of providing a joint perspective on Departmental goals, language, strategic decision making, resource prioritization, program execution and procedures for solving problems across internal boundaries to foster trust and confidence among its components. The Department of Homeland Security should explore expanding the Federal Law Enforcement Training Center's role to include developing education and training requirements for a Homeland Security Professional.

The next chapter will analyze the Department of Homeland Security's partnering capability at the Federal level, specifically those that impact the synchronization of the homeland security enterprise, interagency planning and liaison and demonstrate the benefits of creating an integrating element within the Department.

---

[40] U.S. Joint Chiefs of Staff, *America's Military*, 5.

CHAPTER 4: BUILDING PARTNERING CAPABILITY

Overview

Successful partnering requires mutual trust and cooperation to foster relationships among all of the stakeholders and the interagency. Currently, no single office or component has been charged with the responsibility to foster partnerships among all of the stakeholders in the homeland security enterprise. The complex task of coordination within the Interagency often occurs in an ad-hoc manner and on an emergency basis with no formal process for conducting interagency operations.[1] A recent Government Accountability Office report states that, "the department has failed in taking steps to forge effective partnerships and strengthen the sharing and utilization of information."[2] The accountability for fostering these partnerships resides within each of the components. What this means is each component is empowered to develop its own agreements with select partners.

The Department of Homeland Security must remodel its organizational architecture to include the creation of a new structure to serve as a focal point for building partnership capability across the interagency. Within the Joint Staff, the Directorate for Strategic Plans and Policy: Interagency Planning Branch has the lead for interagency coordination. By examining this directorate in the Joint Staff, the Department of Homeland Security can learn ways to integrate its homeland security activities to enhance interagency cooperation. There are several reasons for integrating

---

[1] Professor L. Erik Kjonnerod, "Organizing the Stovepipes: Interagency thru WOG-WON to Whole of Planet," Presentation at the Center of Applied Strategic Learning, Fort McNair, Washington D.C., July 2011.

[2] Diane Barnes, "Organizational Problems Persist at DHS: Auditors," *Global Security Newswire*, September 8, 2011, under "Daily News on Nuclear, Biological & Chemical Weapons, Terrorism and Related Issues," http://www.nti.org/gsn/article/organizational-problems-persist-at-dhs-auditors/ (accessed August 6, 2012).

the Department's homeland security activities that include: synchronizing efforts within the homeland security enterprise, and assimilating plans and operations across the mission areas.

Synchronizing the Homeland Security Enterprise

The type of security challenges facing our Nation has evolved over the past decade. Relying exclusively on the capabilities of one organization to deal with the threats from terrorism, cyber-attacks, pandemics and catastrophic natural disasters is no longer sufficient. Because of the advances in technology, information, and intelligence, society requires a collaborative approach to bring together various elements of the Homeland Security enterprise found within the Federal, State, and local governments, as well as public and private organizations. The nature of this challenge demands the Homeland Security Enterprise operate as a fully integrated team across a broad range of disciplines. As previously discussed, the core capabilities include planning, public information sharing and warning, and operational coordination.[3] A current goal of the Department is to "enhance its intelligence, information sharing and integrated operations by instituting a mechanism to integrate the DHS's intelligence elements, increasing operational capability and harmonizing operations with Federal, State, local, territorial, tribal, non-governmental, private sector, and international partners."[4] Success is best achieved through shared responsibilities, cooperation, communications and coordination as seen in the interaction between the Department of Homeland Security and State and Major Urban Area Fusion Centers.

---

[3] U.S. Department of Homeland Security, *National Preparedness Goal*, First Edition, Government Printing Office (Washington D.C., 2011), 2.

[4] U.S. Department of Homeland Security, *Department of Homeland Security Strategic Plan, Fiscal Years 2012-2016*, Government Printing Office (Washington, D.C., 2012), 27.

At the State level, the Department of Homeland Security has achieved shared responsibility through 77 State and Major Urban Area Fusion Centers.[5] Fusion centers are defined as focal points "within the state and local environment for the receipt, analysis, gathering, and sharing of threat-related information between the federal government and state, local, tribal, territorial (SLTT) and private sector partners."[6] Fusion centers are important because they are designed to ensure unity of purpose and help build a consensus across various agencies and among partners. These State and Major Urban Area fusion centers are established, managed and controlled "with support from federal partners in the form of deployed personnel, training, technical assistance, exercise support, security clearances, and connectivity to federal systems, technology, and grant funding."[7] The Department's Office of Intelligence and Analysis (I&A) is the lead agency for "developing partnerships and helping facilitate the two-way flow of timely and accurate information authorized by law on all types of hazards."[8]

Unlike its relationships with State and Major Urban Area Fusion Centers, the Department of Homeland Security's relationship with the Interagency is conducted in a more ad hoc manner with over 100 agencies located within 12 Federal departments. The Department of Homeland Security has centralized locations where operational elements are integrated such as the National Operations Center, the Secretary's Crisis Action

---

[5] United States, Information Sharing: Department of Homeland Security Has Demonstrated Leadership and Progress, but Additional Actions Could Help Sustain and strengthen Efforts, U.S. Government Accountability Office (GAO-12-809), Government Printing Office (Washington, D.C., 2012), 3.

[6] U.S. Department of Homeland Security, "State and Major Urban Area Fusion Centers," Department of Homeland Security, http://www.dhs.gov/state-and-major-urban-area-fusion-centers (accessed December 31, 2012).

[7] Ibid.

[8] U.S. Department of Homeland Security, Department of Homeland Security: Interaction with State and Local Fusion Centers Concept of Operation, Government Printing Office (Washington, D.C., 2008), 4.

Team, the National Response Coordination Center and the National Cybersecurity and Communications Integration Center. However, there is no focal point within the Department to promote an information sharing environment and coordination among the Federal stakeholders. According to Laudon, one of the major challenges today is the flow of information across the entire enterprise.[9] Figure 10 provides a visual depiction of Laudon's management system model applied to the information sharing process that spans across the Department of Homeland Security hierarchy and outside of the Department.

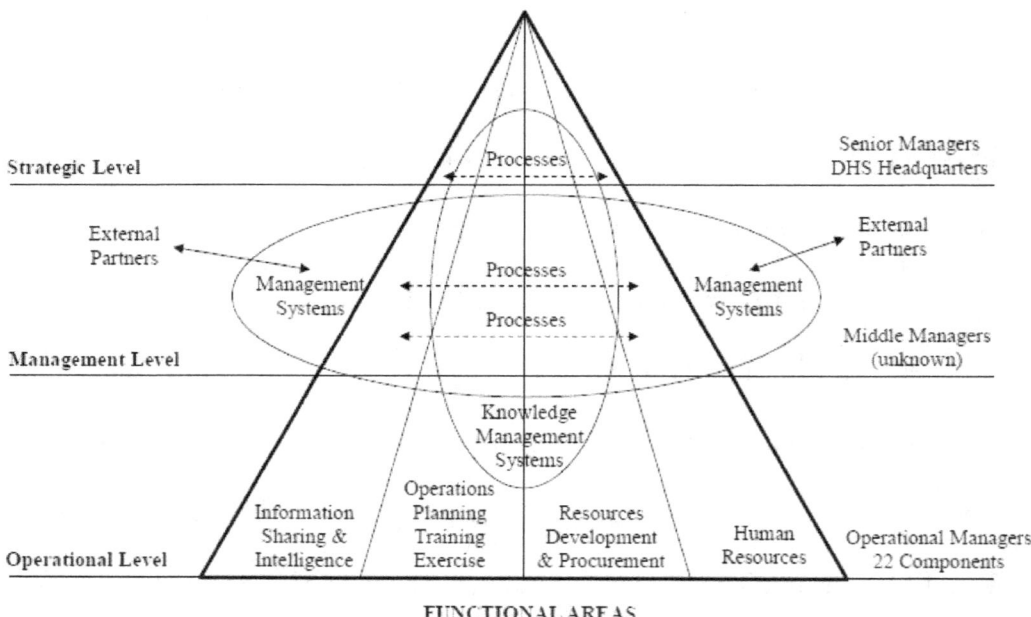

Figure 10. A Depiction of Information System internal and external to DHS.[10]

Similar to Figure 5, this figure shows a pyramid divided into three hierarchical management levels with the four common functional areas listed along the bottom. The two ovals in the center of the pyramid depict the areas normally associated with information sharing and external communication within an organization. Viewing the

[9] Kenneth C. Laudon, and Jane P. Laudon, *Management Information Systems: Managing the Digital Firm*, Ninth Edition (New Jersey: Pearson Prentice Hall, 2006), 54.
[10] The author's illustration of Laudon's model applied to DHS heirarchy.

Department of Homeland Security hierarchy using Laudon's model brings into question what organization or component serves as the integrating element within the organization.

An information sharing environment is one which "combines policies, procedures, and technologies linking the resources (people, systems, databases, and information) of Federal, State, local, and tribal entities and the private sector"[11] needed to share, access, and collaborate among users to protect against terrorism, secure our borders, and respond to disasters of all types. Interagency coordination requires consistent participation in planning, training and operations for the purposes of identifying policy gaps, leveraging resources and bridging the differences in organizational culture.[12] The lack of an adequate information sharing environment and interagency coordination can lead to poor productivity, muddled processes, and even a delay in action. Successful coordination of these efforts requires a collaborative process which is understandable across a wide range of Federal stakeholders.

Interagency Planning

The Department of Homeland Security has articulated that planning is an essential capability required to secure the homeland.[13] However, it lacks the national planning expertise to be effective at all levels of the government because planning staffs are normally smaller within the interagency. Planning requires integration across all five

---

[11] United States, *Department of Homeland Security: Federal Efforts Are Helping to Alleviate Some Challenges Encountered by State and Local Information Fusion Centers,* U.S. Government Accountability Office (GAO-08-35), Government Printing Office (Washington, D.C., October 2007), 2.

[12] U.S. Joint Chiefs of Staff, *Decade of War: Enduring Lessons from the Past Decade of Operations,* Vol I, Joint and Coalition Operational Analysis, Government Printing Office (Washington, D.C., 2012), 25.

[13] Department of Homeland Security Strategic Plan, Fiscal Years 2012-2016, 24.

mission areas[14] to enable the synchronization of Federal, State, local, and tribal homeland security efforts. Effective planning informs decision making at all levels by providing leaders and managers with a common understanding and appreciation of resource programming and budgeting requirements. As the Department of Homeland Security mission grows, the headquarters element begins to lose its capacity to coordinate and integrate homeland security activities due to a shortage of trained and experienced planners. United States Coast Guard Admiral (Retired) Thad W. Allen testified, "The Department has struggled to evolve an operational planning and mission execution coordination capability."[15] As a result, new mission requirements are pushed down to the components by the Department's headquarters to lead homeland security planning efforts. For example, the FEMA was tasked to lead planning efforts among organizations such as OSD-Policy, the Federal Bureau of Investigation, and State emergency managers from Florida to develop the *National Preparedness Description*[16] which they shaped to brief the White House staff. What this means is the FEMA, as component organization, is responsible for formulating strategic policy.

Effective planning within an organization entails a comprehensive approach towards the integration of different plans to form a total system. No single component or agency has the personnel, system, and discipline to lead this effort. Within the Joint Staff, the J-5 Strategic Plans and Policy Directorate is responsible for ensuring Departmental planning efforts are integrated with the Combatant Commands. Likewise,

---

[14] Prevent, Protect, Mitigate, Respond, and Recover.

[15] Thad W. Allen, Admiral (Retired) United States Coast Guard, "The Future of Homeland Security," *FDCH Congressional Testimony* (July 12, 2012): Military & Government Collection, EBSCOhost, 3, (accessed July 31, 2012).

[16] The National Preparedness Description is one of the requirements for Presidental Policy Directive-8.

the Joint Staff integrates internal and external Interagency planning efforts into the Department of Defense at the Joint Staff J-5 level. Internal Interagency coordination is accomplished by the Joint Staff J-5 through plans updates and reviews, while external Interagency coordination is achieved by sending joint staff planners to work with other departments and agencies such as the FEMA's National Operations Center. The benefit of integrating Interagency planning at the mid-management level is it allows for better planning and allocation of available resources, leading to improved work flow and operational efficiencies not typically found within a stove piped component organization.[17]

Department of Defense planners sent to the Interagency normally have the experience and depth of knowledge necessary for valuable contribution to the planning effort. This is not the case in many Federal departments and agencies because they do not have the resources to accommodate a large number of planners on their staff. In the aftermath of Hurricane Katrina and the continued threat of terrorism, President G.W. Bush signed Executive Order 13424[18], *National Security Professional Development*, which initiated a program to develop interagency National Security Professionals by the means of common training, education, and professional experience opportunities.[19] The intent of the National Security Professional Development program is to develop a cadre of professionals who possess the leadership skills, knowledge, and experience that transcends multiple government organizations. The author supports the Department of Homeland Security's initiative to develop these National Security Professionals and

---

[17] QMI - SAI Global, "Integrated Management Systems," SAI Global Limited, http://www.qmi-saiglobal.com/registration/management/Default.asp?language=english (accessed February 18, 2013).

[18] Signed by President G.W. Bush on May 17, 2007.

[19] U.S. Department of Homeland Security, *National Preparedness Report*, Government Printing Office (Washington, D.C., 2012), 71.

understands the resources challenges associated with their training and education. Like the proposed Homeland Security Professional, the National Security Professionals need to be integrated into the Department at the mid-management level as a means to harmonize Departmental methods and processes.

Interagency Liaison Office

Homeland Security is an endeavor that requires a "whole of government" approach that integrates a wide range of government capabilities. By far the largest and most capable of our government departments is the Department of Defense. By law, the Department of Defense has a limited role in expending resources and efforts on affairs within the United States. Homeland Security Presidential Directive-5, *Management of Domestic Incidents* recognized the need for cooperative action between the Department of Defense and the Department of Homeland Security to enhance the ability of the U.S. to provide defense support of civil authorities for domestic incidents by establishing a single, comprehensive national incident management system.[20]

At the request of the Department of Homeland Security Executive Secretary, the Department of Defense agreed that the Office of the Assistant Secretary of Defense for Homeland Defense and America's Security Affairs will provide liaison officers to the Department's headquarters element to facilitate information sharing for defense support of civil authorities response, as well as assist in providing situational awareness to senior Department of Homeland Security and White House leadership. The authority for providing support to the Department of Homeland Security is outlined in the 2004 DoD-DHS Memorandum of Agreement governing Department of Defense personnel support to

---

[20] George W. Bush, "Homeland Security Presidential Directive/HSPD-5 Management of Domestic Incidents," White House Office of the Press Secretary, http://www.fas.org/irp/offdocs/nspd/hspd-5.html (accessed July 30, 2012).

Department of Homeland Security. Over time, this MOA has become outdated, not integrated and not representative of the current liaison structure that supports the Department of Homeland Security. In due course, other Department of Defense components such as the Joint Staff J34, North American Aerospace Defense Command/ U.S. Northern Command, U.S. Pacific Command, U.S. Southern Command, U.S. Special Operations Command, U.S. Transportation Command, U.S. European Command, the National Guard Bureau, U.S. Army Corps of Engineers, and the National Geospatial-Intelligence Agency provided their own liaison officers to the Department of Homeland Security Headquarters and its components in a disaggregated fashion for coordinating functions and activities in support of interagency operations. Likewise, other interagency partners such as the Department of Health and Human Services, the Department of Transportation, and the Federal Bureau of Investigation provide liaisons to the Department of Homeland Security in the same "ad hoc" manner. The problem with this existing state of affairs is liaisons are getting lost within the Department of Homeland Security's organizational structure. A way for the Department to address its liaison issue is similar to that of the Department of State. Within the Department of State, the Office of Plans, Policy and Analysis has integrated a Department of Defense global political-military policy liaison team to interact with the Department on matters pertaining to planning and military activities.[21]

Summary

This chapter offered insight into the complexity of building partnership capability within the Interagency, specifically the Homeland Security Enterprise, by examining

---

[21] U.S. Department of State, "Office of Plans, Policy and Analysis," Department of State, http://www.state.gov/t/pm/ppa (accessed October 19, 2012).

three reasons for integrating the Department's homeland security activities. First, the nature of homeland security requires the Homeland Security Enterprise that operates as a fully integrated team across a broad range of disciplines. This is important because information exchange should not occur for the first time in the middle of a crisis situation. Success is best achieved through shared responsibilities, cooperation, communications and coordination which occurs on a daily basis as seen in the interaction between the Department of Homeland Security and State and Major Urban Area Fusion Centers. However, there is no structure to serve as a focal point within the Department of Homeland Security to promote information sharing environment and coordination among the Federal stakeholders. The author suggests that this common entry point into the Department of Homeland Security should occur at the mid-management level to ensure a unity of effort among all stakeholders.

Second, interagency coordination requires consistent participation in planning, training, and operations for the purposes of identifying policy gaps, leveraging resources, and bridging the differences in organizational culture.[22] It also allows all stakeholders to gain a common understanding of the issues before it becomes a large problem. The benefits of integrating Interagency planning at the mid-management level is it allows for better planning and allocation of available resources, leading to improved work flow and operational efficiencies not typically found within a stove piped component organization.[23] Additionally, the author supports the Department of Homeland Security's initiative to develop its personnel by the means of Executive Order 13424, *National Security Professional Development*; however, the author suggests these professions need

---

[22] U.S. Joint Chiefs of Staff, "Decade of War," 25.
[23] QMI - SAI Global, "Integrated Management Systems."

to be integrated at the mid-management level to harmonize Departmental methods and processes.

Finally, Homeland Security is an endeavor that requires a "whole of government" approach that integrates a wide range of government capabilities. As such, liaisons serve as a means to gain access to these capabilities by getting key players in their parent organizations involved early in the planning process. The Department of Homeland Security cannot afford to wait until a crisis happens to begin to develop these relationships. A way for the Department of Homeland Security to address its liaisons is similar to that of the Department of State by providing an administrative coordinating body within the Department to host collaboration and integrations efforts. The author suggests that this integration should occur at the mid-management level or action officer level.

In the next chapter the author will introduce the newly proposed Department of Homeland Security hierarchy after providing the reader with a historical review of the challenges the Department of Defense faced before it became an integrated organization. Then the author will describe the roles and functions of the newly proposed Homeland Security Integration Element and explain its potential benefits for the Department of Homeland Security Headquarters and its components.

CHAPTER 5: THE NEW HOMELAND SECURITY INTEGRATION ELEMENT

Overview

To set the stage for outlining of the roles and functions of the Homeland Security

Integration Element within Department of Homeland Security, the author will begin by

briefly examining the DoD's hierarchy and those organizations and agencies responsible

for providing a unity of effort among the Armed Forces, including their history,

organizational structure and the Department's relationship with the Department of

Homeland Security. Then, the author will propose the reorganization of the Department

of Homeland Security hierarchy before introducing the Homeland Security Integration

Element.

The Department of Defense

The history of the Department of Defense dates back to Article II of the U.S.

Constitution that designates the President as Commander in Chief with executive powers

to raise armies and to provide for a Navy. In 1789, Congress enacted legislation creating

the Department of War, the Department of State, and the Department of Treasury which

through working together formed the basis for National defense. [1] The first Secretary of

the Department of War, General Henry Knox, served as the commander for both U.S.

land and naval forces.[2] Although there were calls to separate the Navy from the Army,

"considerations of expense and sectional benefits and rivalries among states continued to

postpone any such decision." [3] In response to the pirating of American merchant ships

---

[1] Dr. Frank N. Trager, "The National Security Act of 1947: Its Thirtieth Anniversary," *Air University Review* (November-December 1977), 1, http://www.airpower.au.af mil/airchronicles/aureview/1977/nov-dec/trager.html (accessed December 13, 2012).

[2] Ibid.

[3] Ibid.

along the Barbary Coast, in 1798, Congress established a new "cabinet-level Department of the Navy, separate from the War Department." [4] The War and Navy departments were responsible for their own development.

In the nineteenth century emerging new technologies such as the railroad, the telegraph, quick fire artillery, the machine gun and repeating rifle; and advancements in steel and armor, and in land and sea transport, led to an increased emphasis on a holding defense. Periodically throughout the Civil War and the Spanish-American War, the two military cabinet-level departments displayed a level of joint teamwork in their planning and execution of operations to maneuver into an adversary's rear to gain a decisive victory. "However, instances of confusion, poor inter-Service cooperation and lack of coordinated, joint military action had a negative impact on operations in the Cuban campaign of the Spanish-American War."[5]

With the emergence of the U.S. as a global power following the Spanish-American War came new responsibilities that required a more effective and efficient military. As such in 1903, Secretary of War Elihu Roots instituted several major reforms in the military establishment to include: the implementation of a system of military education; services of supply; the Chief of Staff and General Staff of the Army; the promotion of better operational integration of the Regular Army and Militia; and, the creation of a Joint Army and Navy Board to address "all matters calling for cooperation of the two Services."[6] Unfortunately, Secretary's Roots reforms did not correct all of the issues. Within the Army, the Regulars were suspicious of Militia competence. Equally,

---

[4] Ibid.
[5] National Defense University, *The Joint Staff Officer's Guide: Academic Year 2012-2013*, Joint Forces Staff College, Government Printing Office (Norfolk, 2012), 1-3.
[6] Trager, "The National Security Act," 1.

the Militia display bitterness towards what they deemed as undue federal encroachment of state rights. This continuous friction between parties within the Army prevented the development of mutual understanding and unity of effort of working towards the common goal of national security.[7] This distrust led to the establishment of a standing volunteer federal force, the U.S. Army Reserve, to act separate of the State Militia, which eventually became the U.S. Army National Guard. Likewise, "the Joint Board[8] accomplished little, because it could not direct implementation of concepts or enforce decisions, being limited to commenting on problems submitted to it by the secretaries of the two military departments."[9]

Lessons learned from World War I lead to the development of the National Defense Act of 1920 which presented Congress with an opportunity to reorganize the military by establishing the Air Corps as a separate branch within the War Department and the first recommendation to consolidate the two departments under one cabinet officer; however, no action was taken.[10] During the reorganization debates of 1933, "the Joint Board is unable to recommend an organization for a Department of National Defense that would be more efficient or more economical than the present separate departmental organizations."[11] In the late 1920's, within the War and Navy Departments there were ongoing conflicts over the development and planning of *Operation Orange*, the plan to defend U.S. territory in the Pacific Ocean. While the War and Navy Departments were trying to build a consensus for "formulating concepts of warfare

---

[7] United States Army, The Reserve Components of the United States Military, with Particular Focus on the Reserve Component of the United States Army, The Army National Guard and United States Army Reserve, Army Force Management School, Case GOVT 08-8074, Government Printing Office (Fort Belvior, 2008).

[8] Refers to the Joint Army and Navy Board established in 1903 by President Theodore Roosevelt.

[9] National Defense University, *Joint Staff Officer's Guide,* 1-3.

[10] Ibid, 1-4.

[11] Ibid.

around ground and sea forces", other thinkers within the Air Corps pushed to advance the concept of air warfare to support to both the land and sea components.[12] The fundamental idea of combining the land, air and sea capabilities planted the seed of "jointness". The seeds of "jointness" will begin to take root prior to the end of World War II with issues arising around the "retention of air power in the Navy, maintenance of a separate Marine Corps, and the form and responsibilities of the new Department of the Air Force."[13]

After World War II, the strategic environment changed with the rise of Communism as the primary threat to the survival of the Nation. New demands were placed on the military that called for a stronger unification of efforts which could be accomplished by consolidating the War and Navy departments under a single cabinet-level secretary. "World War II demonstrated that modern warfare required combined and integrated operations by land, sea, and air forces."[14] As such, Congress passed legislation that "set the stage for a major overhaul of the military establishment known as the National Security Act of 1947."[15]

> The National Security Act of 1947 unified the [Military] Services under a single department. In 1949, the National Security Act was amended to change the name of the NME to the Department of Defense and to recognize it as an executive department. Today, [the Secretary of Defense] is the principal assistant to the President for all matters relating to the Department of Defense. He has nearly plenary authority, direction, and control of the entire department. Moreover, the Goldwater-Nichols DOD Reorganization Act of 1986 makes clear his position in the operational chain of command.[16]

---

[12] Michael Eliot Howard and Basil Henry Liddell Hart. The Theory and Practice of War: Essays Presented to B.H. Liddell Hart on His Seventieth Birthday (New York: Praeger, 1965), 225.

[13] Trager, "The National Security Act of 1947: Its Thirtieth Anniversary."

[14] National Defense University, *Joint Staff Officer's Guide*, 1-4.

[15] Ibid.

[16] Ibid.

The results this legislation caused sweeping change in how the Department would function in the future. It brought to an end some of the elements of inter-service rivalry and forced the Services to work together to achieve a unity of effort. For over 65 years, the Department of Defense Architecture has served as a good model for structuring and integrating capabilities within a large organization.

Department of Defense Hierarchy and Capabilities

The Department of Defense is composed of the Office of the Secretary of Defense (OSD), the Office of the Chairman of the Joint Chiefs of Staff (CJCS) and the Joint Staff (JS), the Military Departments, the Unified Combatant Commands, the Office of the Inspector General, and 18 Defense Agencies and 10 Field Activities. Figure 11 provides a depiction of the current Department of Defense Hierarchy.

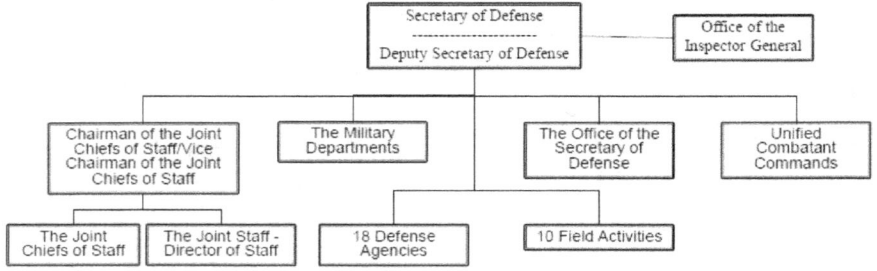

Figure 11. Department of Defense Organizational Chart[17].

Within this organizational structure the Office of the Secretary of Defense provides oversight of the Department's functions; the Office of the Chairman of the Joint Chiefs of Staff and the Joint Staff provide unified strategic direction and serve as a focal point of integration for all of the Military Departments; the Military Departments provide

---

[17] U.S. Department of Defense, "Organizations and Functions of the Department of Defense," Department of Defense, 1, http://odam.defense.gov/omp/Functions/Organizational_Portfolios/Organization_and_Functions_Guidebook.html (accessed March 10, 2013).

manning, equipping, training; and the Unified Combatant Commands are responsible for executing military missions within their geographical areas of responsibly.

The Joint Staff Roles and Functions

The National Security Act of 1947 established the Joint Staff as a permanent agency under the Joint Chiefs of Staff.[18] The Joint Staff is organized into eight directorates to "assist the Chairman of the Joint Chiefs of Staff in accomplishing his responsibilities for the unified strategic direction of the combatant forces; their operation under unified command; and for their integration into an efficient team."[19] The offices and organizations within the Joint Staff are composed of personnel from all four Military Services and civil servants, managed by the Director of the Joint Staff (DJS).[20] Figure 12 provides a depiction of the current Joint Staff Hierarchy.

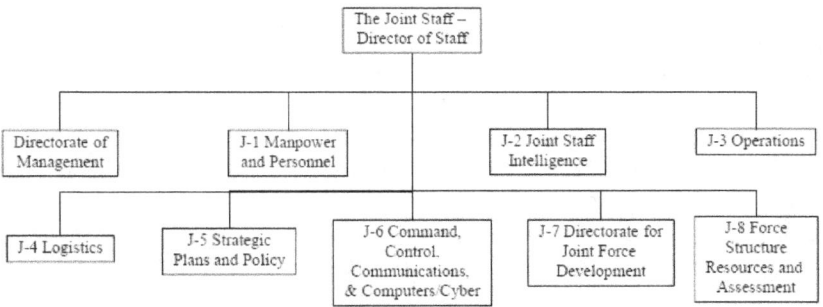

Figure 12. The Joint Staff Organizational Chart[21].

A brief description of the directorates activities are as follows.

> *Directorate of Management* provides assistance to the Chairman of the Joint
> Chiefs of Staff (CJCS) and Joint Staff through management, planning, and
> direction of support activities, including correspondence administration, budget
> and finance, action management and archiving, information technology, services,
> resources, and all aspects of staff and information security.[22]

[18] National Defense University, *Joint Staff Officer's Guide*, 1-3.

[19] U.S. Department of Defense, "Organizations and Functions of the Department of Defense."

[20] United States Code, *Title 10 of the United States Code*, Government Printing Office (Washington, D.C., 1971), 613.

[21] U.S. Department of Defense, "Organizations and Functions."

[22] U.S. Department of Defense, "Directorate of Management," Department of Defense, http://www.jcs.mil/page.aspx?id=15 (accessed March 10, 2013).

The *J-1 Manpower and Personnel Directorate* provides manpower and personnel advice support to the CJCS.[23]

The *J-2 Directorate for Intelligence* is the national-level focal point for crisis intelligence support to military operations, indications and warning intelligence in the Department of Defense, and Unified Command intelligence requirements.[24]

The *J-3 Operations Directorate* moves military forces, conducts detailed operational briefings to the national leadership, and serves as the operational link between the warfighting commanders-in-chief and the National Command Authority.[25]

The *J-4 Logistics Directorate* provides logistics advice to the CJCS.[26]

The *J-5 Directorate for Strategic Plans and Policy* is the focal point for assisting the CJCS in current and future military strategy, planning guidance, and policy; politico-military advice and policies; military positions on projected and ongoing international negotiations; and interagency coordination within these areas.[27]

The *Director J-6* represents the Joint Warfighter in support of the command, control, communications, and computers/cyber (C4) requirements validation and capability development processes while ensuring joint interoperability.[28]

The *Director Joint Force Development (DJ7)* provides support to the CJCS and the Joint Warfighter through joint force development, in order to advance the operational effectiveness of the current and future joint force.[29]

The *J-8 Directorate for Force Structure Resources and Assessment* develops capabilities, conducts studies, analysis, and assessments, and evaluates plans, programs, and strategies for the CJCS.[30]

---

[23] U.S. Department of Defense, "J-1 Manpower and Personnel," Department of Defense, http://www.jcs.mil/page.aspx?id=16 (accessed March 10, 2013).

[24] U.S. Department of Defense, "J-2 Joint Staff Intelligence," Department of Defense, http://www.jcs.mil/page.aspx?id=17 (accessed March 10, 2013).

[25] U.S. Department of Defense, "J-3 Operations," Department of Defense, http://www.jcs.mil/page.aspx?id=18 (accessed March 10, 2013).

[26] U.S. Department of Defense, "J-4 Logistics," Department of Defense, http://www.jcs.mil/page.aspx?id=19 (accessed March 10, 2013).

[27] U.S. Department of Defense, "J-5 Strategic Plans and Policy," Department of Defense, http://www.jcs.mil/page.aspx?id=20 (accessed March 10, 2013).

[28] U.S. Department of Defense, "J-6 Directorate for Command, Control, Communications, & Computers/Cyber," Department of Defense, http://www.jcs mil/page.aspx?id=21 (accessed March 10, 2013).

[29] U.S. Department of Defense, "J-7 Directorate for Joint Force Development," Department of Defense, http://www.jcs mil/page.aspx?id=22 (accessed March 10, 2013).

[30] U.S. Department of Defense, "J-8 Force Structure Resources and Assessment," Department of Defense, http://www.jcs mil/page.aspx?id=33 (accessed March 10, 2013).

The Joint Staff is heavily involved in the dialog and information exchange among the Office of the Secretary of Defense, the Military Services and the Combatant Commands. The key functions of the Joint Staff are to:

(a) Provide credible advice and options to the SECDEF and President;
(b) Ensure flexibility to adjust to the fluid environment in which the Department of Defense is operating, including strategy, policy and planning, and resource allocation;
(c) Provide credible facts and decisions to the SECDEF and President, participate in the PPBS process, including the formal and informal processes;
(d) Assist in setting requirements' priorities.[31]

One of the priorities of the Department of Defense is to provide capabilities to the Department of Homeland Security in times of crisis.

Department of Defense relationship with Department of Homeland Security

The birth of the Interagency Community grew out of the passing of the National Security Act of 1947 and the establishment of the National Security Council that occurred after World War II as interagency planning became a critical factor in meeting national objectives.[32] By law, the Department of Defense has a limited role for applying its resources and efforts in support of domestic issues.

Today, the Department of Defense provides defense support of civil authorities (DSCA) to the Department of Homeland Security and other organizations for special events, disaster relief, counterdrug support, civil disturbance, Chemical, Biological, Radiological, Nuclear, or high yield Explosive (CBRN) incident management, and executing homeland defense operations plans.[33] DSCA is comprised of two mission sets:

---

[31] Leslie Lewis, *Analytic Architecture for Joint Staff Decision Support*, for U.S. Department of Defense and Joint Staff,. Rand, National Defense Research Institute (Santa Monica, California, 1995), 44.

[32] National Defense University, *Joint Staff Officer's Guide*, 1-5.

[33] United States, Homeland Defense DOD Needs to Take Actions to Enhance Interagency Coordination for Its Homeland Defense and Civil Support Missions: Report to Congressional Requesters, U.S. Government Accountability Office (GAO-10-364), Government Printing Office (Washington, D.C., 2010), 2.

homeland defense and civil authorities. Civil authority is secondary to the homeland defense mission. By definition, Homeland Defense is "the protection of U.S. sovereignty, territory, domestic population, and critical defense structure against external threats", whereas civil support is "the overarching term for Department of Defense's support to U.S. civil authorities for domestic emergencies, designated law enforcement, and other activities."[34] The Department of Defense possesses the organic capabilities to respond to a widespread emergency or event. Some of these capabilities not found in any other government agency include immediate access to a large quantity of manpower and equipment, specialized explosive ordnance disposal teams, CBRN assets, and airborne capabilities. Within the Department, the Office of the Assistant Secretary of Defense for Homeland Defense and Americas' Security Affairs, the Joint Staff, the National Guard Bureau, U.S. Northern Command & North American Aerospace Defense Command (NORTHCOM & NORAD), and other Unified Combatant Commands are responsible for close coordination with other federal departments and agencies that have homeland security responsibilities and functions.[35]

Proposed Department of Homeland Security support Architecture

The Department of Homeland Security has seen several reorganizations to its organizational structure and functions. This brings into question whether the Department is structurally sound or could be better organized along functional lines as it stands today. Today, many of the Department of Homeland Security components would prefer an organization model similar to that of the Department of Justice whose component agencies (the Federal Bureau of Investigation, the Drug Enforcement Administration, the

---

[34] Ibid, 1.
[35] Ibid, 3.

Bureau of Alcohol, Tobacco, Firearms and Explosives) are autonomous and have little headquarters-level integration.[36] The primary advantage of Department of Justice organizational model is it allows a component the ability to respond quickly to a need and helps its employees develop better managerial skills.[37] However, the disadvantage of this model is that there can be redundant effort and competition for resources, between components.[38] So, given the nature of Department of Homeland Security's mission coupled with the size of the organization, the author thinks the Department of Justice model is not the best fit for the restructuring of the DHS's Architecture.

The Department of Defense model integrates it components through centralized headquarters structures, functional organizations, and commands. Within the Department's structure, direction is provided by the Secretary of Defense/Office of the Secretary of Defense and the Chairman of the Joint Chiefs of Staff/Joint Staff. This relationship is designed to ensure the adequate integration of the planning and budget processes. The Joint Staff "provides stability and efficiency, which is very important in large and complex organizations, because everyone [needs to] use similar processes."[39] This structure also allows a large organization to take advantage of an economy of scale.

The author proposes that the adaption of a DoD-like model including a Homeland Security Integration Element (the Joint Staff model) would go far to address the three previously stated critical issues that need to be addressed by the Department of Homeland Security: Improved coordination, communication and collaboration throughout the

---

[36] U.S. Department of Justice, "Agencies," Department of Justice, http://www.justice.gov/agencies/index.html (accessed January 9, 2013).
[37] Lisa Magloff, "Advantages & Disadvantages of the Structure of an Organization," *Houston Chronicle*, under "Small Business," http://smallbusiness.chron.com/advantages-disadvantages-structure-organization-2767.html (accessed January 9, 2013).
[38] Ibid.
[39] Ibid.

homeland security enterprise; integration of internal resources management activities; and work environment and workforce enhancement. This reorganization proposal would set up the Department of Homeland Security well for integrating internal DHS operations and facilitating interagency coordination and collaboration with the goal of building a unity of effort across the government departments.

Proposed Department of Homeland Security Hierarchy, Capabilities and Relationships

The reorganization of the Department of Homeland Security would involve the establishment of a Homeland Security Integration Element and the consolidation of 10-direct reporting component agencies into the Headquarters. The Homeland Security Integration Element will oversee a wide range of activities and support functions including strategic operations and planning, intelligence and analysis, resource management, training and exercising, heath affairs and liaison.

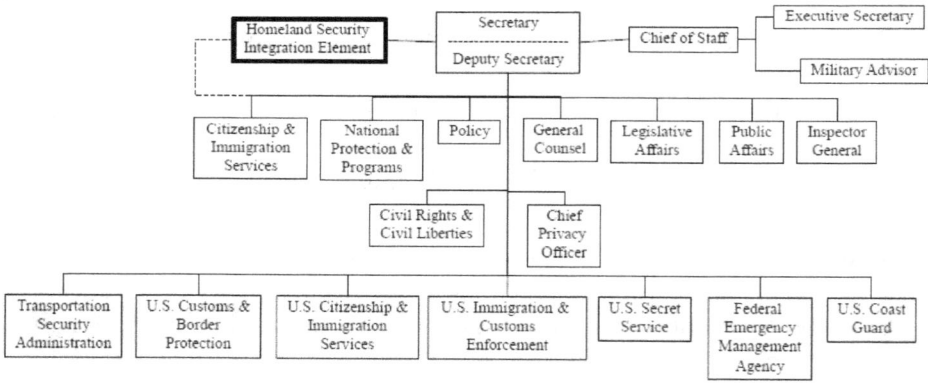

Figure 13. Proposed Department of Homeland Security Organizational Chart.[40]

Figure 13 provides a depiction of the proposed Department of Homeland Security Hierarchy. The offices and organizations within the Homeland Security Integration Element will be composed of personnel and functions from all of the Department's

---

[40] The author's illustration of the proposed DHS organizational chart.

components and agencies, managed by the Director of the Homeland Security Integration Element. The Director of the Homeland Security Integration Element will serve as an advisor to the Secretary, provide unified strategic direction to the Department's components and agencies, and serve as a point for integration of capabilities for its interagency partners.

Proposed Homeland Security Integration Element Architecture, Roles and Functions

The Homeland Security Integration Element will have five principle components to support the Director of the Homeland Security Integration Element: The Office of the Director of Staff, the Directorate of Management, which includes several functional offices, the Directorate of Intelligence, the Directorate of Operations, Plans and Exercise, and the Directorate of Resource Development and Assessment. Figure 14 provides a depiction of the newly proposed Homeland Security Integration Element Hierarchy.

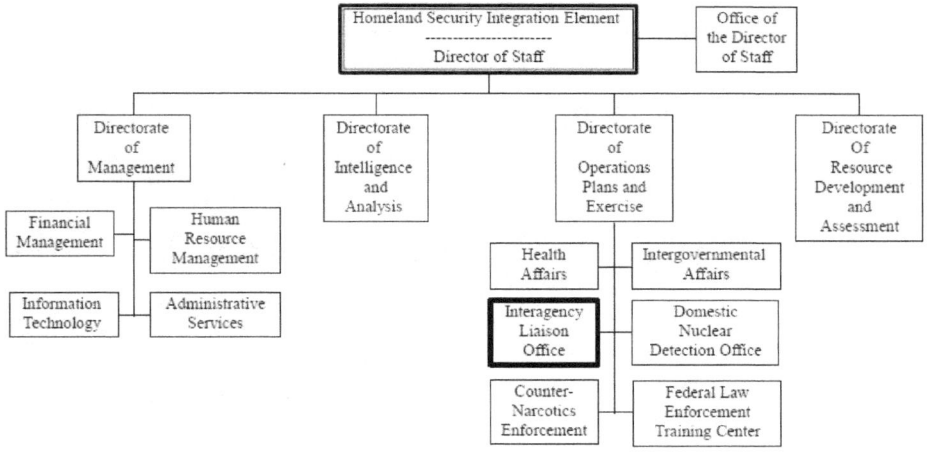

Figure 14. Proposed Homeland Security Integration Element Organizational Chart.[41]

The *Office of the Director of Staff* will oversee the Department's effort to integrate all the activities within the organization. The front office staff will accept, manage, and respond

---

[41] The author's illustration of the proposed Homeland Security Integration Element organizational chart.

to tasks from the Headquarters element and the component heads to receive, update, transmit, and track actions requiring joint integration within the Department.

The *Directorate of Management* will serve as the focal point for assisting the Director of the Homeland Security Integration Element, the Headquarters and its components through administrative services, financial management, grant management, human resource management, and information technology activities and support functions.

The *Directorate of Intelligence and Analysis* will serve as the focal point for crisis intelligence support to National Operations Center operations, and indications and warning intelligence in the Department of Homeland Security and its components.

The *Directorate of Operations, Plans and Exercises* will serve as the focal point for assisting the Director of the Homeland Security Integration Element and the Headquarters and its components in current and future operations and planning, international security cooperation, interagency coordination, exercise and training, and deriving joint doctrine and joint education requirements. This new hierarchy also establishes an Interagency Liaison Office to integrate Federal, State, local, territorial, tribal, non-governmental, private sector, and international partners' homeland security activities.

The *Directorate of Resource Development and Assessment* will serve as the focal point for Resource Management, Planning, Programing and Budgeting as well as Technology Development and Assessment for joint procurement and integration of future science and technology capabilities.

The Homeland Security Integration Element directorates will be staffed by a select number of functional civil service employees from the Department's components. The sub-directorates will be staffed with their current civil service structure.

Proposed Authority and Relationships

The Homeland Security Integration Element will serve under the exclusive authority, direction and control of the Deputy Secretary of Homeland Security. The Homeland Security Integration Element will perform the aforementioned duties described above in the Proposed Homeland Security Integration Element roles and functions section and assist the Deputy Secretary of Homeland Security as required. To facilitate interagency relationships, the Interagency Liaison Office will host liaisons from other Federal departments and agencies. Liaisons will provide the Department with subject matter expertise and direct lines of communication back to their parent organizations with the intent of integrating the development of strategy and policy, the planning of homeland security activities, and the sharing of resources and operational information.

Summary

Like the Department of Defense, the Department of Homeland Security is a large organization with multiple components and agencies. Whereas the Department of Defense capabilities are derived from its Military Departments and integrated within the Joint Staff, the Department of Homeland Security capabilities remain within each component. This means there is no unified strategic direction, and that both external and internal organizations may engage multiple components and agencies to complete an action or even procure a new system. As a result, the Department of Homeland Security can learn from the Department of Defense's experiences and potentially leap forward some 60 years in maturing its organization. The Homeland Security Integration Element will serve as a multidisciplinary organization that integrates expertise from across the Headquarters, its components, and interagency partners. The proposed Homeland Security Integration Element will allow the Headquarters staff to focus on policy formulation, representation and oversight; while, offering the components strategic direction, resource integration, and prevent the unnecessary duplication of efforts in coordination and combined operations. The Homeland Security Integration Element will be formed with almost a "zero sum" change to the existing Department of Homeland Security structure, by combining similar functions and personnel found within the Headquarters and its components.

RECOMMENDATIONS AND CONCLUSION

Significant conclusions from the study

This study offered insight into the complexities of the Department of Homeland Security mission, providing evidence that the Department's current organizational Architecture is in the need of change. This need for change is being driven by our declining resource environment influenced by factors such as sequestration, shrinking budgets, and continuing resolutions that require program restructuring to create better efficiencies at lower cost. Reduced resourcing will lead to more tensions among the 22 components. For the Department of Homeland Security to resolve these tensions will require a balancing act to determine where the Department is willing to take risk when linking its strategy to resources. Likewise, effective execution of Homeland Security often requires the expertise and capabilities of multiple Departments and agencies with differing policy, authority, planning requirements, and funding constraints. The nation cannot afford to wait until a crisis happens to test the robustness of the relationships between Departments and agencies. Thus, the time is now for the Department of Homeland Security to remodel its organizational Architecture to better address the deficiencies and challenges in internal management and interagency coordination and collaboration to build a unity of effort across the homeland security enterprise. Specific recommendations are as follows:

First, the Department needs to determine a way to integrate its internal resources management activities. This can be achieved with the establishment of a Homeland Security Integration Element to enable the integration of internal management systems among the 22 components agencies. The Homeland Security Integration Element will improve the Department's efficiency by serving as a single, central point for management between the senior leadership at the Strategic level and the 22 component agencies at the Operational level. As such, the Homeland Security Integration Element will focus on creating "jointness" at all three levels of management activities that include the strategic integration and oversight of component activities, the operational coordination for acquiring common technology platforms, and the functional integration of centralized guidance in areas such as planning, common doctrine development, and combined operations to achieve the desired outcomes.

Second, the Department needs to build a cohesive DHS culture so its workforce can perform more efficiently and effectively. The Homeland Security Integration Element will merge the management, intelligence and analysis, operations and plans, and resource development and assessment directorates of 10 direct reporting component agencies under one directorate to integrate their related set of functions and processes to enhance the efficiency of the Department as a whole. An essential aspect of the Homeland Security Integration Element is the integration of a cadre of skilled personnel in various areas such as acquisition management, planning and human resources from across the 22 component agencies. The integration of these skilled personnel will serve as a first step towards building trust, improving transparency, cooperation and communication among the 22 component agencies. In situations where resources are limited, the Homeland Security Integration Element provides a forum for open-discussion and conflict resolution to effectively resolve budget issues. When the Secretary of Homeland Security begins to adopt the advice and recommendations of this integrated staff, DHS will begin to develop a new ethos that emphasizes partnering, collaboration, and "One-DHS" mentality.

As Secretary Napolitano begins to develop her vision for DHS 3.0, there is an opportunity for the Department and its components to reexamine their five overarching core values and its potential effects on recruiting their future workforce. Likewise, the Department's leadership has the opportunity to reshape its cultural boundaries by the means of institutionalizing a joint education system to build capacity for future leaders within the Department. In order for the Homeland Security Integration Element to achieve a unity of effort, its staff must be supported with professional mentors. This requires the integration of National Security Professionals (who understand how the interagency works) and Homeland Security Professionals (who understand how the Department works) who are educated on both National Security and Departmental goals, strategic decision-making, resource prioritization, program execution, and procedures for solving problems to foster trust and confidence within the Department and among the stakeholders in the Homeland Security Enterprise.

Finally, the Department needs to improve the way it integrates (coordinate, communicate, and collaborate) it capabilities with other stakeholders throughout the homeland security enterprise. This can be achieved with the establishment of an Interagency Liaison Office within the Homeland Security Integration Element to enhance partnership and collaboration within the interagency. The Interagency Liaison Office is a means for getting key players in external organizations involved early in the planning and information sharing process. Its primary purpose is to get the right people involved at the right time and level for interagency planning, collaboration, decision making, and execution to take place. Developing these personnel relationships will be a key to the Department's success in gaining access to the best information available when bridging the gaps between authorities, funding, and priorities with other stakeholders. Furthermore, the Interagency Liaison Office will also serve as a point of integration for all negotiation, development, and maintenance of memorandums of understanding or memorandums of agreement that promote collaboration and formal partnership between departments and agencies.

Policy Recommendations

The Department of Homeland Security should immediately implement the steps necessary to establish the Homeland Security Integration Element. This will require the Department of Homeland Security to seek Congressional approval for combining 10-direct reporting component agencies under one directorate. Within the Homeland Security Integration Element, the Department must establish an Interagency Liaison Office. In addition, the Department should seek approval for the creation of a Director for the Homeland Security Integration Element. Once approved, the Department can recode positions that support the relocation of certain skilled civil service personnel from across the components. Then, the Department should seek to reprogram resources to co-locate the 10-direct reporting component agencies together in a future location. At this point, the Department of Homeland Security should explore expanding the Federal Law Enforcement Training Center's role to include developing education and training requirements for a Homeland Security Professional and then, immediately determine the requirements needed to fund the National Security Professional program.

Suggestions for further research

It is recommended that further research be undertaken in the following areas. First, there is a need to study ways to de-conflict the overlap of authorities, policies, and procedures between departments and agencies. Second, there is a need to study how to resolve the duplication of Congressional oversight provided by 86 committees and subcommittees. Third, there is a need to study the impact of U.S. public expectations in times of crisis to gain an understanding of what capabilities are required to protect the American people and to become better stewards of the taxpayers' dollars.

Concluding Remarks

In conclusion, this study has shown that after a decade of existence the Department of Homeland Security faces major challenges in orchestrating a unity of effort, both internally and across the whole-of-government, to protect the homeland from threats to our nation's way of life. The cost of failure is too high. In her testimony to the House Judiciary committee, Secretary Janet Napolitano said, "Threats against our nation, whether by terrorism or otherwise, continues to exist and evolve. And DHS must continue to evolve as well."[1] Unfortunately, DHS does not have the same luxury of time to mature as the Department of Defense. It took the Department of Defense over 200-years to mature as an organization, including 60-years to achieve the level of "jointness" they experience today. Therefore, the time is now for the Department of Homeland Security to remodel its organizational Architecture to include the creation of a Homeland Security Integration Element to act as a focal point for strengthening its internal management and partnering capability.

---

[1] Janet Napolitano, Secretary of United States Department of Homeland Security. "DHS Oversight," *FDCH Congressional Testimony* (July 12, 2012): Military & Government Collection, EBSCOhost, 17 (accessed July 31, 2012).

BIBLIOGRAPHY

ARTICLES FROM A PRINT MAGAZINE

Chanley, Virgina A. "Trust in Government in the Aftermath of 9/11: Determinants and Consequences." *Political Psychology* 23, no. 3 (September 2002): 469-483.

Van Es, Roeliene. "Public Opinions on Security and Civil Liberties in America after the Terrorist Attacks of September 11, 2001." *Social Cosmos* 3, no. 1 (2012), 118-123.

ARTICLES FROM AN ONLINE MAGAZINE

Ballenstedt, Brittany. "Task Force recommends measures to improve DHS culture." *Government Executive*. February 13, 2007. http://www.govexec.com/management/2007/02/task-force-recommends-measures-to-improve-dhs-culture/23725/ (accessed August 3, 2012).

Barnes, Diane. "Organizational Problems Persist at DHS: Auditors." *Global Security Newswire*. September 8, 2011. http://www.nti.org/gsn/article/organizational-problems-persist-at-dhs-auditors/ (accessed August 6, 2012).

Magloff, Lisa. "Advantages & Disadvantages of the Structure of an Organization." *Houston Chronicle*. http://smallbusiness.chron.com/advantages-disadvantages-structure-organization-2767.html (accessed January 9, 2013).

Trager, Frank N. "The National Security Act of 1947: Its Thirtieth Anniversary." *Air University Review*. November-December 1977. http://www.airpower.au.af.mil/airchronicles/aureview/1977/nov-dec/trager.html (accessed December 13, 2012).

BOOKS

Daft, Richard L. *Organization Theory and Design.* Mason, Ohio: South-Western Cengage Learning, 2008.

Harvey, Don, and Donald R. Brown. *An Experiential Approach to Organizational Development: Six Edition.* New Jersey: Prentice Hall, 2001.

Howard, Michael Eliot and Basil Henry Liddell Hart. *The Theory and Practice of War: Essays Presented to B.H. Liddell Hart on His Seventieth Birthday.* New York: Praeger, 1965.

Laudon, Kenneth C., and Jane P. Laudon. *Management Information Systems: Managing the Digital Firm; Ninth Edition.* New Jersey: Pearson Prentice Hall, 2006.

Schein, Edgar H. *Organizational Culture and Leadership*. San Francisco: Jossey-Bass, 1992.

Thompson Jr., Arthur A., A.J. Strickland III, and John E. Gamble. *Crafting and Executing Strategy: The Quest for Competitive Advantage*. Boston: McGraw-Hill, 2005.

CONGRESSIONAL HEARINGS

Allen, Thad W. Admiral (Retired) United States Coast Guard. "The Future of Homeland Security." *FDCH Congressional Testimony* (July 12, 2012): Military & Government Collection, EBSCOhost (accessed July 31, 2012).

Carper, Tom. Senator. U.S. Senate. Senate Homeland Security and Governmental Affairs, Committee. "The Future of Homeland Security." *FDCH Congressional Testimony* (July 12, 2012): Military & Government Collection, EBSCOhost (accessed July 31, 2012).

Collins, Susan M. Ranking Member. Senate Homeland Security and Governmental Affairs, Committee. "The Future of Homeland Security." *FDCH Congressional Testimony* (July 12, 2012): Military & Government Collection, EBSCOhost (accessed July 31, 2012).

Harman, Jane. Congresswoman. U.S. House of Representatives. Senate Homeland Security and Governmental Affairs, Committee. "Senator Joseph I. Lieberman holds a hearing on Homeland Security Department's Roles/Missions." *FDCH Political Transcripts (n.d.):* Military & Government Collection, EBSCOhost (accessed July 31, 2012).

Lieberman Joseph I. Senator, Chairman. "Senator Joseph I. Lieberman holds a hearing on Homeland Security Department's Roles/Missions." *FDCH Political Transcripts (n.d.):* Military & Government Collection, EBSCOhost (accessed July 31, 2012).

Napolitano, Janet. Secretary of United States Department of Homeland Security. "DHS Oversight." *FDCH Congressional Testimony* (July 12, 2012): Military & Government Collection, EBSCOhost (accessed July 31, 2012).

CONGRESSIONAL RESEARCH SERVICE REPORTS

Congressional Research Service. *Federal Emergency Management Policy Changes after Hurricane Katrina: A Summary of Statutory Provisions, by the Congressional Research Service, March 2007*. Washington, D.C.: Government Printing Office, 2007.

Congressional Research Service. *Department of Homeland Security FY2013 Appropriations, by the Congressional Research Service, October 2012.* Washington, D.C.: Government Printing Office, 2012.

LECTURES

Kjonnerod, L. Erik, Professor. "Organizing the Stovepipes: Interagency thru WOG-WON to Whole of Planet." Presentation at the Center of Applied Strategic Learning, Fort McNair, Washington D.C., July 2011.

Waugh, William L. Jr. "The Future of Homeland Security." Presentation at the FEMA Higher Education Conference, Emmitsburg, MD, June 7-9, 2005.

OTHER

Lewis, Leslie. *Analytic Architecture for Joint Staff Decision Support* for the U.S. Department of Defense and Joint Staff. Rand, National Defense Research Institute. Santa Monica, CA, 1995.

Military Leadership Diversity Commission. *Department of Defense Core Values.* Military Leadership Diversity Commission Issue Paper 6. Arlington, VA, December 2009.

United States Code. *Title 10 of the United States Code.* Government Printing Office. Washington, D.C., 1971.

PRESIDENTIAL PUBLICATION

United States President (Obama). *National Security Strategy.* Washington DC: Government Printing Office, May 2010.

PUBLICATIONS OF GOVERNMENT DEPARTMENTS AND AGENCIES

National Defense University. *The Joint Staff Officer's Guide: Academic Year 2012-2013.* by Joint Forces Staff College. Government Printing Office. Norfolk, VA, January 2012.

United States. *Department of Homeland Security: A Comprehensive and Sustained Approach Needed to Achieve Management Integration: Report to Congressional Requesters.* U.S. Government Accountability Office (GAO-05-139). Government Printing Office. Washington, D.C., March 2005.

United States. *Department of Homeland Security: Actions Taken Toward Management Integration, but a Comprehensive Strategy Is Still Needed.* U.S. Government Accountability Office (GAO-10-131). Government Printing Office. Washington D.C., November 2009.

United States. *Department of Homeland Security: Oversight and Coordination of Research and Development Should Be Strengthened.* U.S. Government Accountability Office (GAO-12-837). Government Printing Office. Washington, D.C., September 2012.

United States. *Department of Homeland Security: Federal Efforts Are Helping to Alleviate Some Challenges Encountered by State and Local Information Fusion Centers.* U.S. Government Accountability Office (GAO-08-35). Government Printing Office. Washington, D.C., October 2007.

United States. *Department of Homeland Security Progress Made and Work Remaining in Implementing Homeland Security Missions 10 Years After 9/11: Report to Congressional Requesters.* U.S. Government Accountability Office (GAO-11-881). Government Printing Office. Washington D.C., 2011.

United States. *The Federal Response to Hurricane Katrina: Lessons Learned.* The White House Office of the Press Secretary. Government Printing Office. Washington D.C., February 2006.

United States. *Homeland Defense DOD Needs to Take Actions to Enhance Interagency Coordination for Its Homeland Defense and Civil Support Missions: Report to Congressional Requesters.* U.S. Government Accountability Office (GAO-10-364). Government Printing Office. Washington, D.C., March 2010.

United States. *Homeland Security: Information Sharing Responsibilities, Challenges, and Key Management Issues.* U.S. Government Accountability Office (GAO-03-1165T). Government Printing Office. Washington D.C., May 2003.

United States. *Information Sharing: Department of Homeland Security Has Demonstrated Leadership and Progress, but Additional Actions Could Help Sustain and strengthen Efforts.* U.S. Government Accountability Office (GAO-12-809), Government Printing Office. Washington, D.C., September 2012.

United States. *National Security: An Overview of Professional Development Activities Intended to Improve Interagency Collaboration.* U.S. Government Accountability Office (GAO-11-108). Government Printing Office. Washington, D.C., November 2010.

United States. *Quadrennial Homeland Security Review: Enhanced Stakeholder Consultation and Use of Risk Information Could Strengthen Future Reviews.* U.S. Government Accountability Office (GAO-11-873). Government Printing Office. Washington D.C., September 2012.

U.S. Army. *The Reserve Components of the United States Military, with Particular Focus on the Reserve Component of the United States Army, The Army National Guard and United States Army Reserve.* Army Force Management School, Case GOVT 08-8074. Government Printing Office. Fort Belvoir, VA, September 2008.

U.S. Department of Homeland Security. *2011 Federal Employee Viewpoint Survey: Empowering Employees.* U.S. Office of Personnel Management. Government Printing Office. Washington D.C., 2011.

U.S. Department of Homeland Security. *Capital Planning and Investment Control Guide: Version 4.0.* The Office of the Chief Information Officer. Government Printing Office. Washington D.C., May 2007.

U.S. Department of Homeland Security. *Department of Homeland Security: Interaction with State and Local Fusion Centers Concept of Operation.* Government Printing Office. Washington, D.C., December 2008.

U.S. Department of Homeland Security. *Department of Homeland Security Strategic Plan, Fiscal Years 2008-2013.* Government Printing Office. Washington, D.C., September 2008.

U.S. Department of Homeland Security. *Department of Homeland Security Strategic Plan, Fiscal Years 2012-2016.* Government Printing Office. Washington, D.C., October 2012.

U.S. Department of Homeland Security. *FY 2013 Budget in Brief,* Government Printing Office. Washington, D.C., October 2012.

U.S. Department of Homeland Security. *Homeland Security Act of 2002,* P.L. 107-296, 116 Stat. 2135. Government Printing Office. Washington, D.C., November 2002.

U.S. Department of Homeland Security. *Homeland Security Risk Management Doctrine: Risk Management Fundamentals.* Government Printing Office. Washington D.C., April 2011.

U.S. Department of Homeland Security. *Implementing Recommendations of the 9/11 Commission Act of 2007.* P.L. 110-53, 121 Stat. 266. Government Printing Office. Washington, D.C., August 2007.

U.S. Department of Homeland Security. *National Preparedness Goal,* First Edition. Government Printing Office. Washington D.C., September 2011.

U.S. Department of Homeland Security. *National Preparedness Report.* Government Printing Office. Washington, D.C., March 2012.

U.S. Department of Homeland Security. *Quadrennial Homeland Security Review Report*. Government Printing Office. Washington, D.C., February 2010.

U.S. Department of Homeland Security. *Report of the Homeland Security Culture Task Force*. Government Printing Office. Washington D.C., January 2007.

U.S. Joint Chiefs of Staff. *America's Military-Professions of Arms White Paper*. Joint Chiefs of Staff. Government Printing Office. Washington, D.C., February 2012.

U.S. Joint Chiefs of Staff. *Decade of War: Enduring Lessons from the Past Decade of Operations*, Vol I, Joint and Coalition Operational Analysis. Government Printing Office. Washington, D.C., June 2012.

U.S. Joint Chiefs of Staff Instruction. *Chairman of The Joint Chiefs Of Staff, Combatant Commanders, Chief, National Guard Bureau, And Joint Staff Participation in the Planning, Programming, Budgeting And Execution Process*. CJCSI 8501.01B. Washington DC: Joint Chiefs of Staff, August 21, 2012.

U.S. Joint Chiefs of Staff Instruction. *Joint Officer Management Program Procedures*. CJCSI 1330.05. Washington DC: Joint Chiefs of Staff, May 1, 2008.

WEBSITE

Bush, George W. "Homeland Security Presidential Directive/HSPD-5 Management of Domestic Incidents." Administration of George W. Bush, 2003. http://www.gpo.gov/fdsys/pkg/PPP-2003-book1/pdf/PPP-2003-book1-doc-pg229.pdf (accessed July 30, 2012).

Bush, George W. "Homeland Security Presidential Directive/HSPD-8: National Preparedness." Administration of George W. Bush, 2003. http://www.gpo.gov/fdsys/pkg/PPP-2003-book2/pdf/PPP-2003-book2-doc-pg1745.pdf (accessed August 17, 2012).

Cherry, Kendra. "Psychology: Hierarchy of Needs; The Five Levels of Maslow's Hierarchy of Needs." About.com. http://psychology.about.com/od/theoriesofpersonality/a/hierarchyneeds.htm (accessed December 1, 2012).

Federation of American Scientist. "Information Sharing Environment (ISE)." Federation of American Scientist. http://www.fas.org/irp/agency/ise/index.html (accessed December 31, 2012).

Thomas, Michael. "Emergency Managers endorse removing FEMA from DHS."
   Lighthouse Worldwide Solutions.
   http://hspolitics.wordpress.com/2008/11/20/emergency-managers-endorse-
   removing-fema-from-dhs/ (accessed December 7, 2012).

QMI - SAI Global. "Integrated Management Systems." SAI Global Limited.
   http://www.qmisaiglobal.com/registration/management/Default.asp?language=en
   glish (accessed February 18, 2013).

U.S. Department of Defense. "Directorate of Management." Department of Defense.
   http://www.jcs.mil/page.aspx?id=15 (accessed March 10, 2013).

U.S. Department of Defense. "J-1 Manpower and Personnel." Department of Defense.
   http://www.jcs.mil/page.aspx?id=16 (accessed March 10, 2013).

U.S. Department of Defense. "J-2 Joint Staff Intelligence." Department of Defense.
   http://www.jcs.mil/page.aspx?id=17 (accessed March 10, 2013).

U.S. Department of Defense. "J-3 Operations." Department of Defense.
   http://www.jcs.mil/page.aspx?id=18 (accessed March 10, 2013).

U.S. Department of Defense. "J-4 Logistics." Department of Defense.
   http://www.jcs.mil/page.aspx?id=19 (accessed March 10, 2013).

U.S. Department of Defense. "J-5 Strategic Plans and Policy." Department of Defense.
   http://www.jcs.mil/page.aspx?id=20 (accessed March 10, 2013).

U.S. Department of Defense. "J-6 Directorate for Command, Control, Communications,
   & Computers/Cyber." Department of Defense.
   http://www.jcs.mil/page.aspx?id=21 (accessed March 10, 2013).

U.S. Department of Defense. "J-7 Directorate for Joint Force Development." Department
   of Defense. http://www.jcs.mil/page.aspx?id=22 (accessed March 10, 2013).

U.S. Department of Defense. "J-8 Force Structure Resources and Assessment."
   Department of Defense. http://www.jcs.mil/page.aspx?id=33 (accessed March 10,
   2013).

U.S. Department of Defense. "Organizations and Functions of the Department of
   Defense." Department of Defense.
   http://odam.defense.gov/omp/Functions/Organizational_Portfolios/Organization_
   and_Functions_Guidebook.html (accessed March 10, 2013).

U.S. Department of Homeland Security. "About DHS." Department of
   Homeland Security. http://www.dhs.gov/about-dhs (accessed July 30, 2012).

U.S. Department of Homeland Security. "Creation of the Department of Homeland Security." Department of Homeland Security. http://www.dhs.gov/creation-department-homeland-security (accessed October 8, 2012).

U.S. Department of Homeland Security. "Department Six-point Agenda." Department of Homeland Security. http://www.dhs.gov/department-six-point-agenda (accessed October 6, 2012).

U.S. Department of Homeland Security. "Presidential Policy Directive/PPD-8: National Preparedness." Department of Homeland Security. http://www.dhs.gov/presidential-policy-directive-8-national-preparedness (accessed July 30, 2012).

U.S. Department of Homeland Security. "Secretary of Homeland Security Janet Napolitano's Third Annual Address on the State of Homeland Security." Department of Homeland Security. http://www.dhs.gov/news/2013/02/26/secretary-homeland-security-janet-napolitano%E2%80%99s-third-annual-address-state-homeland (accessed March 16, 2013).

U.S. Department of Homeland Security. "State and Major Urban Area Fusion Centers." Department of Homeland Security. http://www.dhs.gov/state-and-major-urban-area-fusion-centers (accessed December 31, 2012).

U.S. Department of Homeland Security. "Written testimony of DHS Management Under Secretary Rafael Borras for a House Committee on Homeland Security, Subcommittee on Oversight, Investigations, and Management hearing titled 'Building One DHS: Why Can't Management Information be Integrated?'." Department of Homeland Security. http://www.dhs.gov/news/2012/02/29/written-testimony-dhs-management-under-secretary-house-homeland-security (accessed September 7, 2012).

U.S. Department of Justice. "Agencies." Department of Justice. http://www.justice.gov/agencies/index.html (accessed January 9, 2013).

U.S. Department of State. "Office of Plans, Policy and Analysis." Department of State. http://www.state.gov/t/pm/paa (accessed October 19, 2012).

U.S. Joints Chiefs of Staff. "Director Responsibility Statement." Joint Chiefs of Staff. http://www.jcs.mil/page.aspx?id=13 (accessed December 26, 2012).